A Gift from Bob

Also by James Bowen

A Street Cat Named Bob
The World According to Bob
Bob: No Ordinary Cat
For the Love of Bob
Where in the World is Bob?
My Name is Bob

A Gift from Bob

James Bowen

First published in Great Britain in 2014 by Hodder & Stoughton
An Hachette UK company

First published in paperback in 2015
This paperback edition published in 2020

1

A CIP catalogue record for this title is available from the British Library

ISBN 978 1 529 35761 5

Typeset in Cochin by Hewer Text UK Ltd, Edinburgh
Printed and bound in Great Britain by Clays Ltd, Elcograf S.p.A.

Hodder & Stoughton policy is to use papers that are natural, renewable
and recyclable products and made from wood grown in sustainable
forests. The logging and manufacturing processes are expected to
conform to the environmental regulations of the country of origin.

Hodder & Stoughton Ltd
Carmelite House
50 Victoria Embankment
London EC4Y 0DZ

www.hodder.co.uk

In loving memory of Bob

2006? to 2020

To the Street Cats, Bobites and all the other groups
who have come together thanks to our shared love.

To the Winters Family Clan
In moments that felt hopeless TMB & A always
brought sunshine and warmth to my life.

'"Maybe Christmas," the Grinch thought,
"doesn't come from a store."'

Dr Seuss

'Time spent with cats is never wasted.'

Sigmund Freud

Prologue

London, December 2013

It was still a few weeks before Christmas but inside the swish hotel near Trafalgar Square the party was already in full swing. The huge, mirrored ballroom was buzzing; there must have been more than two hundred people milling around, chatting and laughing. A small army of smartly dressed waiters and waitresses were circulating with trays of champagne, wine and tasty-looking canapés. Everyone was in a festive mood.

The lunchtime gathering had been organised by one of the biggest publishers in London and was dotted with well-known authors. Every now and again I'd see a face that looked familiar, then realise I'd seen them on television or in a newspaper.

To judge by the way they greeted each other with flamboyant hugs and kisses, a lot of the party-goers were old friends. I, on the other hand, barely knew a soul.

A part of me felt a little bit like a gatecrasher, as if I was there on false pretences somehow. Except that I wasn't.

To begin with, the smart, gold-embossed card inviting me and my 'plus one' was still tucked inside my leather jacket, where I intended to keep it as a memento. Also, a few minutes earlier, as everyone had gathered in the room, the hostess of the party, the head of the company, had publicly thanked a few of the authors who had braved the cold weather to be there. One of the names she'd singled out had been mine. Well, mine along with that of my 'plus one' for the day, to be precise.

'And we're really delighted to see James Bowen, accompanied, of course, by his constant companion Bob,' she'd said to loud applause.

Every head in the room had seemed to turn in my direction. If they'd all been staring at me I'd have been overwhelmed with self-consciousness, but fortunately they hadn't. As so often happened these days, all eyes had actually focussed on a point somewhere above my shoulders and the handsome, ginger cat who was perched there, staring out imperiously, like the captain of a galleon, surveying all before him. He was the star attraction. As usual.

It was no exaggeration to say that Bob had saved my life. When I'd met him six years earlier he'd been a stray, lying injured in the hallway of my block of flats in north London. His arrival had marked a huge turning point in my troubled life. At the time I'd been a recovering heroin addict, struggling to complete a methadone programme. I was twenty-eight years old and had spent the best part of a decade sleeping rough and in homeless shelters or sheltered accommodation. I was lost. Caring for Bob had given me the impetus and incentive I needed to turn my life around. I'd done that, firstly by busking and selling the homeless magazine *The Big Issue*, but also by weaning myself off drugs.

Bob was by far the most intelligent and resourceful cat I'd ever encountered. Our time together on the streets of London had been eventful but also hugely cathartic. Each day it seemed like he gave me direction, purpose, companionship and, well, a reason to smile.

His impact had been so great that I'd been approached to write a book about our adventures together. When it had been published in March 2012, I'd not expected it to sell more than a hundred copies if I was lucky. Instead, to my utter amazement, it had become a bestseller, not just in the UK but around the world. Since then I'd written a second book about my life on the streets with Bob, as well as a children's picture book imagining Bob's life before we met. Between them they had sold more than one million copies in the UK alone. It had been this success that had earned Bob and myself an invitation to this particular gathering.

With the speeches over, the party really got into top gear. The waiters were great with Bob and provided me with a couple of bowls so that I could lay out some food and some special cat milk that I'd brought along with me. Bob was always a people magnet and today was no exception. Partygoers kept coming up to us wanting to take a picture of Bob and say hello. They would congratulate me on my success and ask about my future plans. For the first time in my life I actually had some and I shared them happily. I was particularly proud of the work I was now doing for homeless and animal charities. I felt like I was giving back to people who had given me a lifeline when I'd really needed it. When people asked me how I planned to spend Christmas, I told them how Bob and I, along with my best friend Belle, were going to treat ourselves to a nice West End show and a couple of meals at smart restaurants.

'Must be very different from the Christmases

you spent a few years ago,' one lady said to me. I just smiled and nodded.

'Just a little.'

At one point there was a small, very well-heeled queue waiting to meet Bob. No matter how hard I tried, I could never quite get used to this kind of attention, even though it was becoming common-place. A few days before this, for instance, I had spent a day at a London hotel making a film for Japanese television. Back in Japan, I later learned, actors were reconstructing my life with Bob for a dramatisation of our story that was part of this tele-vision programme. I couldn't quite get my head around that.

A few months before this we had been on ITV receiving an award at the UK's first televised National Animal Awards, watched by an audience of millions. In many ways my life resembled a dream. I was doing things that I wouldn't have imagined possible, almost on a day-to-day basis. I lived in a constant state of wanting someone to pinch me.

As it turned out, the biggest 'pinch me' moment of the Christmas party came right at the end. We had been there for a couple of hours when the party began to break up. Bob was looking tired in any case, so I was ready to leave. I had knelt down to attach the lead that Bob wore when we were out on the streets together when I became aware of someone standing behind me.

'I've been meaning to come over. Do you think he'd mind if I gave him a quick hello?' a female voice asked.

'Just a moment, please, I'm just fixing his harness,' I said, turning around and looking up.

I recognised the face immediately. It was the children's author Jacqueline Wilson, a national treasure in the UK and author of dozens of classic children's books.

I'm not usually short of something to say, but I was lost for words. I was really flummoxed. I think I muttered something about how much I admired her, which was true, and how Belle was a huge fan of her most popular character, Tracy Beaker, which was definitely true.

'I have been following your story and I think what the pair of you have achieved is fantastic,' she said.

We chatted a little more as we both headed out of the party and into the foyer of the building. It was such a thrill for me. I'd felt like an outsider, a usurper, but she'd made me feel like I belonged in this world.

As usual, Bob was wearing one of the scarves that he'd been gifted by his many admirers. Stepping out into the late afternoon gloom, I adjusted it so that it protected him from the cold.

'Well that was fun, wasn't it, mate?' I said, feeling a sense of elation that the party had gone so well.

As so often in the past, the streets of London soon snapped me back to reality. The sky was darkening and a cutting wind was blowing down from the direction of Trafalgar Square where I could see the traditional, giant Christmas tree lit up already for the evening.

'Come on, Bob, let's get a black cab,' I said, heading towards the Square.

That was something else that sometimes made me pinch myself. The prospect of taking a taxi had been unthinkable not so long ago. I barely had enough money to pay for a bus some days. Even now I took cabs infrequently. I always felt guilty spending the money, even when, as on this occasion, it was justified. It had been a busy day, Bob was tired and cold and we had to meet Belle near Oxford Circus.

The street was busy with shoppers and people starting to head home after a day's work so it was hard to spot a cab with its yellow light on. I had just failed to flag down the umpteenth taxi when I spotted the familiar red tabard of a *Big Issue* seller on the corner.

I instantly recognised the distinctive bobble hat, gloves and scarf he was wearing. The Big Issue Foundation handed out a cold weather package each winter to those long-term sellers who needed it. The man's bearded, wind-reddened face didn't ring any bells, however. He had long, lank grey hair and was in his fifties probably.

I could see he had a large pile of magazines, which suggested to me he'd either just started his day or he was really struggling to sell them. From experience, I suspected the latter.

I could also tell he was really feeling the cold. He was repeatedly stamping his feet to try to keep the blood flowing and kept blowing into his hands to try to get some warmth into his wind-chilled body.

I walked over and gave him a £20 note. I didn't have any loose coins.

'Cheers, mate,' he said, delighted but also looking a little confused that a random guy had given him that much money. When he offered me the change I just shook my head.

For a moment he weighed me and Bob up. His face was wearing an expression that seemed to be asking, *Why?*

'Really, mate, I know what it's like. I know how cold it gets and just how hard this time of year is. Please take it, I understand the difference a few extra quid can make,' I said.

He had no idea who I was, which was hardly surprising. It wasn't as if I was on television or anything like that.

He looked sceptical, but smiled.

'Trust me, I really do,' I said.

'OK, I'll take your word for it.'

I was just about to head off when he suddenly reached down.

'Oh, wait a minute, mate, here's something for you,' he said, rummaging around in his rucksack.

The Christmas card he produced had a nativity scene on the front. He'd probably picked it up in a pound shop or a charity store. Inside it said, very simply: *Merry Christmas, thank you for your support, Brian.*

'Thanks,' I said. 'Hope you manage to have a good one too.'

I would have stayed to talk a little longer but I was suddenly aware of a taxi approaching with its yellow light on. Bob was getting restless and I needed to get going. The instant I opened the door Bob bounded in, grateful for the warmth. He then curled himself up on the seat alongside me, ready for a well-deserved snooze.

As we pulled away, I turned around and watched Brian melt into the London evening. The red and grey figure had soon become indistinguishable from the blur of coloured lights in Trafalgar Square, but I couldn't shake the image of him – and the simple gesture he'd made – out of my mind. It stirred up a whole array of emotions and memories, some poignant, some happy, others very sad.

It hadn't been so long ago that I had been in exactly the same boat. For more than a decade I too had been an invisible face in the crowd, relying on the kindness of strangers. The last Christmas I'd spent working full-time on the streets was that of 2010, just three years earlier.

As the black cab weaved its way northwards, along Regent Street with its gaudy Christmas window displays and street decorations, my mind flashed back to that year. Life on the streets had always been a struggle, but that Christmas had been particularly tough and testing. Yet I remembered how it had also been filled with important lessons; lessons that, as I dwelled on them again now, suddenly seemed even more precious given the unexpected turn that my life had taken. They were the type of lessons that no amount of money or success could have bought. And, as I prepared for another, very different type of Christmas, I knew they were lessons I must never forget.

Three years earlier
London, Christmas 2010

Chapter 1

Golden Paws

The walk home was slow and painful.

It had been one of the coldest Decembers on record and the day before had seen one of the biggest blizzards in twenty years. Six inches of snow had fallen in a couple of hours. Today the pavement was a shiny, rutted, iron-grey sheet of ice. It was absolutely treacherous. Each time I took a step I wondered whether my luck would hold or whether, instead, I was going to fall flat on my face. To make matters worse, every time I placed my foot down, a sharp, shooting pain worked its way up my right leg.

It had been that leg that had brought me out today. It had been giving me trouble all month and earlier that week my doctor had confirmed what I'd suspected; the pain was a recurrence of a problem I'd suffered for a while, deep vein thrombosis, or DVT, in my upper thigh. A year or so ago I'd spent some time in hospital being treated for it. My doctor told me to take some painkillers, but warned that the best thing to do was to stay in the warm until the end of the Arctic weather.

'The cold basically slows the blood down,' he said. 'So it helps to stay indoors.'

'As if,' I had said to myself at the time. 'It's a week or so before Christmas, there's more snow in London than Siberia. How exactly am I going to eat and heat my flat if I don't go outdoors and do some work?'

Reluctantly, I'd taken his advice for a few days. The weather had been so intense there had been absolutely no way I could venture out. But this afternoon the throbbing had got so bad that I'd had to hobble over to the shops near my block of flats to get some more painkillers. It was a Sunday, and even though Christmas was now just six days away, a lot of the shops were closed. So I'd had to walk further to a little convenience store that had a little pharamacy.

It was normally only a five minute walk home, but the slippery surface meant that today it took twice as long. At one point I felt so unsteady I found myself holding on to the walls and railings as I inched my way along. When I finally reached the door of the block of flats where I had lived for the past four years or so I breathed a huge sigh of relief. It wasn't just that I'd safely negotiated the ice rink that was my road. The wind was so cold it had begun to chill my bones; it felt good to feel the warmth of the building.

Even better, the lift was working. We'd had a fancy new elevator with an electric display fitted earlier in the year. It had been more efficient than the old, hydraulic one which broke down all the time. I had been dreading walking up the five flights of stairs to my flat on the top floor of the building, especially given the nagging pain my leg was giving me.

By the time the lift doors opened on the fifth floor I could feel my mood lightening. The comical sight that greeted me when I walked into my flat raised my spirits further still.

Belle had come over to see us. Belle was, like me, a recovering addict. If her life hadn't taken a similar wrong turn to my own, she could easily have been an artist or designer. She was always creating things from odds and ends she found. As usual at this time of the year, she had decided to make her own Christmas decorations and cards. I could see a few of them neatly stacked alongside her already.

An array of card, glitter, glue, string and ribbons was now spread out on the small coffee table in the living room. It was pretty obvious that Bob had been joining in the fun; the evidence was right there in front of me.

The first thing I noticed was lengths of ribbon everywhere. I spotted little bows on various cards Belle had made and realised Bob must have nabbed the leftover ribbons while she wasn't looking. It was as if he'd tried to tie a bow around the entire flat; there was ribbon on the carpet, over the back of the sofa and even around the television set. He had completely run amok.

That wasn't the only mess he'd made. I noticed a series of glittery, gold paw prints on the carpet and part of the sofa. I could see that they stretched all the way into the kitchen where he'd clearly popped in for a drink from his water bowl. Then I saw a large gold stamping pad open on the table. It didn't take much to put two and two together. He must have somehow dipped his paws into it. I'd heard of *Goldfinger* but this was *Golden Paws*.

Belle was so absorbed in what she was doing that she was oblivious to the fact that Bob had been almost as creative as her.

'I see Bob has had a good time,' I said, taking off my coat and gesturing to the ribbon and paw prints.

She looked non-plussed.

'What do you mean?'

'His paw prints. The ribbon.'

'What paw prints and ribbon?' she said, looking around. 'Oh.'

It didn't take long for the penny to drop. For a moment she looked embarrassed but she was soon convulsed by laughter and couldn't stop giggling for ages.

'Ah bless him. Well you know how he likes to try to get involved,' she said.

Belle loved Christmas and looked forward to it every year. Each year we finished putting up the tree she gave Bob a big hug, as if to celebrate the official start of the countdown to the 'big day'. As far as she was concerned, making a mess with rib-bons and glitter was simply part of the fun. I just shook my head, genuinely mystified.

To judge by his behaviour, not just today but throughout the past week or so, Bob was a big fan of the festive season too. It was the third Christmas I'd spent with him and I'd never seen him more excited.

He had always been fascinated by Christmas trees. Our first one had been a tiny artificial tree that you connected to a USB point on a computer. He loved the twinkling lights and would stare at it endlessly, as if mesmerised. For the past couple of years we'd had a slightly bigger tree. It was nothing

special, just a cheap, black artificial one that I'd
picked up in a local supermarket. It was about
three and a half feet high and sat on top of an old
wooden cocktail cabinet that I'd found in a second-hand shop years ago.

The tree may have been pretty basic compared to
some of the dazzling ones we'd seen displayed
around London in the past weeks, but Bob was
absolutely obsessed with it nevertheless. Belle would
always bug me to put it up at the earliest possible
opportunity in December. The moment it came out
of its box Bob became a bundle of hyperactive
energy. He loved watching it being assembled and
decorated and was very particular about how this
was done. Each year, when I started dressing it up,
he would stand next to me supervising. Some decorations would get his seal of approval, others would
not. An angel at the top of the tree, for instance, was
a non-starter. The previous year, I'd found a silver
fairy in a charity shop that Belle had rather liked but
the moment I placed it at the top of the tree Bob
started reaching up as if to dislodge it. He had car-
ried on until I took it down. He preferred a simple
gold star. So that's what we had again this year.

Bob also liked baubles on the branches of the
tree, rather than ribbons. They couldn't be any old
baubles, of course. They had to be shiny, gold or
red preferably. He liked fairy lights, but they had

to be hung correctly so that they were concentrated at the front of the tree where he could see them.

Every now and again, I would try to put something new up, such as a chocolate ornament or a pine cone. Almost immediately he would reach up with his paw or, failing that, jump up on his hind legs to flick at it or remove it. Belle had tried to put some home-made ribbons up this year but Bob had grabbed at them with his paw and dragged them off almost contemptuously. It was as if he was saying, *How dare you put that rubbish on my Christmas tree.* If Bob wasn't happy sometimes he would simply pull the tree over, sending everything crashing to the floor.

As if this wasn't bizarre enough, he was also really particular about the positioning of the tree. He seemed to like it so that the branches were all separated so that he could see inside it. I had a theory about this. In the run up to the big day, we would start placing small presents under the tree. Bob loved playing with them, sometimes even nudging them off the cabinet so that they fell on to the floor where he ripped them open. In anticipation of this, I actually put up a few empty boxes, simply so he could go through this ritual. My theory was that he hated the idea of not being able to see what presents were lurking at the base of the tree, which was why he would try to move the branches apart if he felt they were clumped together, obstructing his view.

Once the tree was in the right place and correctly decorated Bob would guard it as if it was the most important thing in the entire world. Woe betide anyone who tried to touch or move the tree. If you did he would let out a deep snarl and then reposition it, which was quite something to behold. He would grab a branch with his mouth, then rotate it through a few degrees so that it was aligned at the precise angle he wanted.

This protectiveness could backfire on him at times. He would regularly squeeze himself under the tree, arching his body around its base so as to get a good look around its perimeter. On a few occasions he got himself wedged under the tree so that, when he lifted his back, he tipped it over. It was the same when he pulled it down; it was hilarious to watch. The entire edifice would topple over, sending Bob flying through the air and baubles and other bits and pieces tumbling across the living-room floor. Bob would then chase the loose baubles around, nudging them in a slightly demented way. Of course it was a pain reconstructing the tree so that it was in the perfect position again, but it always made me laugh. That was always an achievement at this time of the year and especially this year.

Times were tighter than they had been for a long time, which was saying a lot for someone who had lived on the breadline for the best part of fifteen years.

The Arctic weather meant that I'd found it almost impossible to go out to work, busking or selling *The Big Issue*, for the past week or so. I'd ventured out a couple of times but had either turned back because of the problems on public transport or given up because it was simply too cold to stand around on the streets with Bob. It had felt good to stay in the warm watching the snow falling while Bob curled up by his favourite radiator, but my confinement had come at a high price.

I lived a hand-to-mouth existence, so the fact that I'd been stuck at home meant that I had virtually no money left. There were times of the year when I could have coped with that more easily, but with Christmas around the corner it was a real frustration.

I liked to get ready for Christmas by buying the bits and pieces I needed for the holiday little by little. In a way, I approached it like Johnny Cash's old song, 'One Piece At A Time', about a man smuggling parts from the factory where he worked to build a motor car. There had been a time, during the darkest days of my drug addiction, when I might have resorted to shoplifting as well, but thankfully those days had long gone. These days I was happy to pay for them, even if it was one at a time. So, over the past couple of weeks, the kitchen had slowly been filling up with the little treats and traditional food and drink that Bob and I liked to share at Christmas. Naturally, there was a healthy supply of Bob's favourite rabbit meals along with several packets of his favourite treats, special cat milk and a few extra goodies ready for him to enjoy come Christmas and Boxing Day. For myself I had bought a small turkey crown and a gammon joint, which were both now safely stored in the tiny fridge-freezer in the kitchen. I'd bought them near their sell-by dates but despite this they had been quite expensive, by my standards at least. I'd treated myself to a small packet of smoked salmon, some cream cheese and a small tub of nice ice cream and I'd also snapped up some brandy butter to have with the Christmas pudding I tended to eat with Belle when she came around on Boxing Day. There was also some orange juice and a half bottle of cheap cava that I was looking forward to popping on Christmas morning.

It wasn't a lavish Christmas by any stretch of the imagination – I probably spent a fraction of what the average family splashed out on presents, food and drink. But as cheap as they were, these things still cost money – and I had hardly any.

I'd been preoccupied with my situation for days now. My mind had been constantly churning through the options I had for making some money, not that there were many of them. With the weather as bad as it was, and forecast to get even worse, I felt like I was trapped in some kind of bad dream. I was a big fan of Tim Burton movies and had noticed in the newspaper that his most famous seasonal film was on TV in a couple of days' time. It summed up my situation perfectly. I was living *The Nightmare Before Christmas*.

As I left Belle to her handicraft and made myself a cup of tea in the kitchen, I was fretting over my situation once more. It must have been obvious because Belle had soon appeared at the doorway with a sympathetic look on her face.

'Come on, Scrooge, cheer up a bit,' she said. 'It's almost Christmas.'

I was tempted to say 'bah, humbug' but just shrugged my shoulders instead.

'Sorry, but I'm afraid the Christmas spirit hasn't quite taken over yet,' I said.

Belle knew me well enough to read my mood – and the probable cause of it.

'I'm sure you'll get some money together before Christmas Eve,' she said, reassuringly.

'We'll see,' I said grumpily.

I took a couple of gulps of my tea then headed

back into the living room. I gathered up the ribbon and started dabbing away at the paw prints with a damp cloth. Fortunately, the marks came out pretty easily. Bob was still padding around the place, leaving a golden trail in his wake. I knew this wasn't healthy for him so I decided I'd better put an end to the fun.

'Come on, buster,' I said, scooping him up. 'Time to give you a wash.'

Belle took the hint and started clearing away her bits and pieces. She looked concerned. She was all too aware of the problems I was facing, in particular the most pressing of them domestically speaking.

'Have you got any gas left to heat some water?'

'No, I'll have to put some in a saucepan and warm it up on the electric hob.'

'OK.'

'Actually, can you just go and check the state of the electric meter too,' I said. 'I haven't looked for a bit. I'm afraid to.'

I wasn't exaggerating.

There had been times in my life when I'd been obsessed by all sorts of things: guitars, science fiction novels, computer games, how I was going to 'score' my next fix when I was an addict. At the moment, however, my greatest obsessions took the form of the gas and electric meters that were positioned near the front door of my flat. I'd been forced to have the meters installed after failing to pay my quarterly energy bills in the past. The meters were charged up by pay-as-you-go cards and both needed regular top-ups at the nearby convenience store. I'd add as much money as I could afford to each but, with energy prices rising all the time, it wasn't cheap. I reckoned it cost on average about £2 to £3 a day to keep both of them going during this cold weather. It didn't take long for it to mount up. The one consolation was that I'd already paid the quarterly rental fee I had to pay for the meters at the beginning of December. But during the past week I'd been trying to keep the flat as warm as possible, which had meant the meters were eating money at a horrendous rate. The consequences had been inevitable.

Both meters had an option which gave you £5 of emergency energy. When you reached this point, you had to insert the card into the meter and hit the E button. It would then make three beeps to let you know that you were on emergency supplies. Once that had run out, however, that was that. It was effectively a loan or overdraft, so until you had repaid the £5 plus any extra debt you had run up you were cut off. A couple of days ago I'd been forced to put both the gas and electric on emergency. I knew I had just £5 left on each before I was disconnected, so from that moment onward my life had become ruled by the noises emanating from the meters – and the complicated timetable that kept them running.

Because people might not be able to top up their cards or keys during the night-time, both meters had what the energy companies liked to call a 'friendly non-disconnect period'. This basically meant that, provided you had some credit at the cut-off time, usually 6 p.m., they didn't disconnect you in the middle of the night or on Sundays when it might be difficult to find a shop open to top up your card or key.

These cut-off times had been my major obsession. At 6 p.m. each day for the past few days I'd breathed a huge sigh of relief when the meter made a soft clicking noise that announced the energy supply wouldn't be cut off until at least 9 a.m. the following morning. When it had done so on Saturday, I'd known that I had that night and all of Sunday guaranteed. I'd known that the earliest the supply could be disconnected was 9 a.m. on Monday morning. Since then I'd been through the same traumatic ritual each morning, watching the clock tick towards 9 a.m., waiting to see if the dreaded beeping of the machine signalled that I'd run out of gas or electric. It wasn't good for my nerves.

Two days ago, I'd heard the gas run out. It meant

that I couldn't have baths and that, more importantly, the gas-fired central heating was out of action. Bob wasn't impressed; it meant that his favourite spot by the radiator in the living room was no longer the toasty little haven that it was normally. I had resorted to using a tiny, electric fan heater which I put on intermittently to heat the living room. It guzzled electricity so I knew I could only use it sparingly though. The rest of the time I either sat in the kitchen, or hid under the duvet on the sofa or in my bedroom. Bob had begun curling up with me, sharing what warmth we could muster between us.

I knew there was a large debt on top of the £5 emergency credit because I'd run it through a whole weekend. So to get the gas up and running again, I worked out that I was going to need somewhere in the region of £15. That was money I didn't have at the moment.

My biggest fear now was that the electric would get disconnected as well. Then I really would be in deep trouble, especially as a lot of the more expensive Christmas stuff I'd accumulated was all in the fridge. If that was cut off it wouldn't take long for the food to spoil and I'd have to throw it all in the dustbin. I doubted whether I'd be able to replace it all, not least because the shelves were getting empty in the supermarkets.

So I knew I had to somehow get out into the world and earn some money. I couldn't let the weather or the pain in my leg be obstacles any longer. It was too depressing and dispiriting – not to mention dangerous, given the way the temperatures were plunging almost on a daily basis. Bob and I could easily freeze if, as predicted, the mercury dropped to ten degrees below zero.

Above all else, however, I wanted this situation sorted out. I didn't want to be constantly listening for the tell-tale 'beep, beep, beep' sounds that signalled the meter switching off. I didn't want to be in permanent dread of having the contents of my fridge defrosting. Just as importantly, I also knew how much Bob and Belle were looking forward to Christmas and I wanted to share in that excitement. They'd helped me so much; the least I could do was repay them with a few happy and carefree days together.

Deep down, I had another even greater motivation. I didn't want a Christmas where I felt like Scrooge, begrudging the festive season's entire existence. I didn't want to appear like the miserable Grinch putting a dampener on everyone else's holiday. I'd had enough of those sorts of Christmases. I'd been playing those roles for far too long.

Chapter 2

The Boy Behind the Curtain

There's an old saying that 'Christmas isn't a season, it's a feeling'. I'm sure it's true. For most people that feeling is one of almost childish joy. Whether it's the sheer excitement and anticipation of Christmas Eve or the warmth of the laughter around the table at Christmas dinner, that feeling is what makes it the happiest time of their year.

For the first thirty or so years of my life, the feeling Christmas stirred in me was very different. I mostly associated it with sadness and loneliness. It was why I usually dreaded it. It was why I had wanted it to simply go away.

My attitude was hardly surprising given the way my childhood and teenage years had unfolded.

I'd been born in Surrey but my parents had separated soon after my arrival in the world. Then, when I was three, my mum and I left England for Australia where she had relatives. She had got a job as a star saleswoman for the photocopying company, Rank Xerox.

I was an only child and our life had been a pretty rootless one; we'd moved from one city to another with my mum's job which meant that I attended a lot of different schools. I didn't really settle in any of them and suffered a lot of bullying as a result. I'd always tried a little too hard to fit in and make friends which obviously made me stand out from the crowd. That was never a good thing at school. In the little town of Quinn's Rock in Western Australia, I'd been stoned by a bunch of kids who thought I was some kind of misfit weirdo. It had left me a nervous wreck.

I spent most of my home life alone as well, which didn't help. My mum worked hard, travelling around Australia and beyond and going to meetings all the time so I was effectively raised by a series of nannies and babysitters. I rarely had company.

This constant moving around meant that we didn't really do the traditional family Christmas. My dad remained in England so he couldn't come and visit but he was very generous with the gifts he sent over. I vividly remember receiving the original Transformers toys one year. I also got sets of walkie-talkies and expensive Matchbox cars. I really appreciated them, but felt even more excited when I was able to speak to my dad on the telephone. To me, hearing his disconnected, slightly echoey voice at the other end of the world was often the highlight of my Christmas.

We did have family in Australia, in particular my mother's brother, my uncle Scott and his family, who we saw on rare occasions when we visited Sydney. We didn't spend the holiday season with them, however. Instead my mother's idea of a Christmas celebration was to spend a lot of money on trips for the two of us. She must have been making quite a bit of money at the time because they were quite lavish affairs. We made at least three trips like this and flew to America, Thailand, Singapore and Hawaii. One year, for instance, we flew east from Australia to Hawaii, passing through the International Date Line. So we were effectively flying back in time. We left on Boxing Day but arrived in Hawaii when it was still Christmas Day.

So I had two Christmas Days. It must have been very exciting and I'm sure I must have had a great time. My mum has often talked to me about our travels, but I remember very little.

The one thing I do recall though is that I spent

a large part of these trips on my own. One year we stopped off in Las Vegas where my mother spent most of the time in the casino, leaving me in the bedroom. There was absolutely nothing for me to do so I just watched television. I wouldn't have minded too much, except for the fact that it was pay-per-view television and I didn't have access to that. So I spent the holiday endlessly watching the only free programme on the hotel's own channel, a preview of *Dolly Parton's Christmas Special*. Can you imagine the nightmare of watching Dolly Parton saying 'Howdy folks' over and over again for hours on end? I still wake up in a cold sweat about that programme every now and again.

We also visited New York. It should have been a really exciting trip, but my mum got a migraine so I had to look after her. I was cooped up in this darkened room for days, or so it seemed. At one point I was so bored, I remember vividly standing on the other side of the drawn curtains, with my face pressed against the glass watching the snow fall on the New York city sidewalk below. It looked absolutely beautiful, like something out a 1950s Hollywood movie. It's about the most magical thing about Christmas that I can recall from my childhood.

There are other, powerful memories. For instance,

I remember on one of the long-haul flights we took I spilled a large glass of orange juice all over the smart blue suit I was wearing. I have no idea how my mother had afforded it, but we were travelling in first class. My suit was so thoroughly soaked that the stewardess had to take me downstairs and back into economy to change into a dressing gown. But when I tried to get back into the first-class lounge they wouldn't let me in. My mum was asleep, so she hadn't realised I was missing. A male steward kept forcefully putting me into a seat in economy. I can still see his face; he looked a little like Barack Obama. He would sit me down then make a grand gesture of closing the curtains that separated economy from first class, closing the Velcro fasteners on them as he did so. It was as if I was being punished for even thinking I belonged in such a rarefied atmosphere.

I will never forget the look of embarrassment on his face when, at the fourth attempt, I managed to sneak through the curtain and slipped back upstairs and into the chair next to my mother, who was just waking up. He couldn't quite believe it when she assured him that I was, indeed, travelling with her. I have often thought about that moment as symbolic of the way my life went after that. It still pretty much summed it up now. No one wanted me spoiling their cozy little world, no one thought

I belonged. I was always the boy on the wrong side of the curtains.

I don't want to sound ungrateful, nor do I want to blame my mother for this. She had plenty of problems of her own and I wasn't always the easiest child, there's no doubt about that. At the time she probably thought that she was doing a good thing, showing me the world and the finer things in it. But from my point of view, it looked very different. To me she was trying to make up for the fact she was never there during the rest of the year. These ostentatious Christmas holidays were simply her way of compensating for that absence. She couldn't see that what I needed was not first-class air travel or five-star hotels. I just wanted to spend some quality time with a mother I hardly knew in a proper family environment. Most of all, of course, I just wanted to be loved.

When I was around ten or eleven, my mum and I moved back to England for a couple of years. Christmas remained a pretty lonely affair, for different reasons this time. Both the Christmases I spent there were memorable in their own ways. I spent the first with my dad and his then wife Sue and my half-sister Caroline, who was then a toddler of around three. It was, probably, the closest I got to a 'normal', 'happy' Christmas in the sense that I was with an extended family, eating, handing out presents, watching television. I really enjoyed the feeling that I belonged in a larger family group. And, of course, it felt great to be with my father at Christmas time, rather than talking to him long distance on the phone. It was a typical family Christmas in other ways too, there were arguments, for instance. I remember my mum buying a baby doll for Caroline at a petrol station on the journey there. The baby was one of those ones that cried *waaah* when you rocked it. Caroline was still very young and I used to encourage her to make a noise just like the doll, much to my dad's annoyance.

'James, cut it out,' he would shout all the time.

Looking back on it, I can see that my father would already have seen me as a rather troubled soul, even at that age. Twelve months later it was an opinion that was shared by others too. I spent the following Christmas being assessed at a mental institution for young people, Colwood Hospital in Haywards Heath, West Sussex.

By that point me and mum clashed a lot. My behaviour was so extreme at times that she had been convinced there was something psychologically wrong with me. One of the doctors I saw had been worried that I had depression so I was put on lithium for a few months. It wasn't a long-term solution, however, so I was sent for assessment.

They tested me for everything from schizophrenia to manic depression and ADHD but failed to come up with a definitive answer to what was wrong with me.

I've blanked out a lot of what happened during my stay at Colwood. That's partly because of what I went through during my period of assessment, but partly too because I was treated with all sorts of drugs. I still have vivid memories of having injections that would send me to sleep. I often wouldn't have a clue where I was when I eventually came round. Sometimes it would happen completely unexpectedly; a doctor would appear at my side with a syringe and I was suddenly losing consciousness. I never resisted, it was scary but I trusted the doctors and wanted my troubles to go away. They didn't, of course.

It's hardly surprising then that the Christmas I spent at Colwood is a real blur. The only thing I recall is my dad taking me out to see a pantomime. That was a happy memory. It must have been Cinderella because I remember the character Buttons throwing out Cadbury's Buttons™, the chocolate sweets, into the audience. I also remember Caroline crying on the way home because her magic fairy wand had broken. It's strange what the mind retains and what it discards.

By the following Christmas we were back in

Australia. My mother was a little homesick but I think she thought the move back would be good for my state of mind too. So with her new partner Nick she decided we'd better get away. But there was no running away from the fact that I was an unhappy child and that she and I didn't get on.

I missed England and my father. I also missed the affection I'd found there. I continued to fight with my mother and Nick, with whom I really didn't get along. Aside from that Christmas with my dad, the warmest memory from our time back in England was of a nurse called Mandy. She was the kindest person I'd ever encountered. She had spent a lot of time with me when I'd been at Colwood Hospital, not just caring for me but talking and listening to me, something that I hadn't really experienced much before.

Back in Australia I adopted a feral cat from a rescue shelter. I really liked the cat and she seemed to really like me too, so I called her Mandy to remind me of a happy time back in the UK.

Otherwise, however, my life in Australia went downhill pretty steadily. I spent time in more institutions, but they only made the situation worse if anything. For a while I'd been in a psychiatric ward in the Princess Margaret Hospital in Perth, Western Australia. When I was nearly seventeen I was put in a place called the Frankston Psychiatric

Unit For Children on the other side of the country, in Victoria. By now I was a real tearaway and was experimenting with drugs. I'd try anything, from glue to medicinal drugs that could give me the highs I craved. There was absolutely nothing else to do in that hospital. It was also my way of escaping from the grim reality of the place.

During my time at Frankston I saw things that I'd not wish on anyone. One day an older inmate who I had befriended, a grungy kind of biker guy they called 'Rev', asked me whether he could borrow my razor. Naively I thought he wanted a shave, but, of course, he didn't. I felt really guilty about that for a long time although fortunately he didn't die. He just needed to make a cry for help.

It's very easy for people to say they never had a stable childhood but in my case, I think that's a pretty true statement. The combination of my parents' separation and a childhood that felt like it was spent constantly on the move, often from one side of the world to the other, made it extremely unstable. Given this, I guess the decline that happened when I arrived back in England at the age of eighteen was almost inevitable. Back in Australia I'd been diagnosed with Hepatitis C, which the doctors ascribed to my drug-taking. I'd cried when they told me that, back then, my life expectancy was no more than ten years. It turned out I had a very strong immune system and was able to survive it but I didn't know that at the time.

I'd headed back to England with a kind of death sentence hanging over me. I'd had ambitions to be a musician but they had come to nought. Instead, I'd drifted from one home to another and eventually one sofa to another and finally on to the street where I spent a time sleeping rough. Once I got there I turned to heroin and other drugs as a means of escape. I took anything that dulled my senses. My life just spiralled downward and downward. Sometimes I shake my head in wonder at how I am still alive.

As a result, Christmas had become even less meaningful to me. It was simply a time of the year that needed to be survived, not enjoyed.

By now, I'd had a couple of Christmases with my father in south London but they weren't brilliant. I didn't really connect with my family any more; I felt that they thought of me as the black sheep, which was a valid point of view. I certainly wasn't the easiest stepson in the world.

As a consequence, Christmas with my dad meant literally turning up on Christmas Eve, staying for Christmas Day then being dropped off at the station on Boxing Day morning. One time I got dropped off only to discover that there were no trains, so I had to walk the four miles or so to

Croydon to get the overground train, which took me the best part of an hour. It had all just underlined what an awful time of the year it was, for me at least.

To be honest, the main reason I went was to get a really decent meal. At that point in my life, good food was a real rarity for me. I was living in sheltered accommodation and earning no money. There were times when I was so desperate I'd even resorted to rummaging in skips at the back of big supermarkets. I really didn't care what I ate as long as it was edible. So I really looked forward to Christmas dinner, to seeing that giant plate of food served up and then being allowed the freedom to pile up another plateful of food as soon as I'd finished.

Given all this, it was hardly surprising that Christmas had meant very little to me even when I began to get my life sorted out. All the things it represented – family, togetherness, kindness, community and charity – simply didn't register with me. While everyone else looked forward to it and enjoyed the build-up, I never understood that excitement at all. I couldn't understand why people spent so much money and got so worked up in anticipation of what, to me, seemed like just another day of the year. I actually viewed it with a sense of foreboding, almost fear.

It was something that Belle, in particular, found hard to comprehend. My friendship with her was, like most things in my life, complicated. We had first met back in around 2002, when I was trying – and failing – to make a name for myself in a band called Hyper Fury. The band had a brief period when we were playing a few gigs around London, especially in Camden. I met her at a club there called The Underworld. I'd been at the bar when she had come up and overheard me talking to another woman about the fact our birthdays were on the day after each other, mine on March 15th and hers on March 16th.

'Oh that's funny,' Belle had chipped in. 'My birthday is March 17th.'

'That's St Patrick's Day,' I'd said. We'd quickly fallen into a conversation.

I'd found her funny and easy to talk to and we had spent the rest of the night chatting.

She had been in a relationship with another guy at the time, but they had been drifting apart. We agreed to meet up a week or so later and really hit it off, so Belle ended her relationship and we became an item.

Belle was a Londoner, born and bred, and was a couple of years younger than me. But even though we'd grown up on the other side of the world from each other our lives had followed very similar trajectories. She had gone through a difficult time at home, in particular the loss of her grandmother who she regarded as her second mother. She had, like me, become a troubled teenager with similar psychological issues. She had been prone to spates of depression and had also developed a drug habit, in her case going from pot to harder and harder drugs. I understood it completely when she said it was her way of blocking out the pain she felt, of escaping a world in which she felt so alone. I knew exactly how she felt. This created a really close bond between us and our relationship briefly blossomed. For a while we shared a flat together.

It had been during that period while we were going out together that Belle had seen at first-hand how and why Christmas meant so little to me. I'd been invited to stay with my stepmother Sue in south London in the run-up to Christmas so I asked Belle to come along too to meet my family. She quickly sensed what a difficult atmosphere there was between us all. There had been lots of arguments, not least over a remark that someone had made about not understanding what a nice, normal girl like Belle was doing with me. This had really angered me.

'Try living my life,' I'd spat back at them.

Belle, on the other hand, was close to her mum and dad and was planning to head back to her home in west London to spend Christmas Day with them. It was a special time of the year for them; they really went to town on the celebrations. On Boxing Day I had been invited over to meet her parents. The atmosphere there could not have been more different; it was very warm and welcoming. Her mum made a huge fuss over me, effectively cooking a second Christmas dinner with all the trimmings. They even bought me a present, which completely threw me. It gave me an inkling of what a big, happy family Christmas could be like.

Unfortunately, our relationship hadn't lasted. At that time in our lives, we were both battling with our personal demons and it was just too difficult. We weren't good for each other in that respect. We'd drifted apart for a little while, but we'd stayed in touch. As the years had passed, we had slowly grown to realise that we were better as friends than as boyfriend and girlfriend. As we'd both dealt with our respective problems, that friendship had deepened into a really close bond that, we both knew, was going to last a long time.

Belle and I got on like a house on fire. We shared a lot of common interests, including cats. When she was a teenager, she had adopted a cat called Poppy from the Cats Protection charity. Poppy had been found in the home of an elderly guy who had offered sanctuary to more than a dozen cats. When he had passed away the cats had all been taken in by the local Cats Protection branch. Poppy had been seven when we met and was still as lively as ever at the age of fifteen. In many ways, Poppy was as important to Belle as Bob was to me. She put a smile on her face even on the darkest days. She was her source of unconditional love.

Given this, it was no surprise that Bob got on really well with Belle. He had always been happy to stay with her when I was ill or not around. In particular, he had stayed at her flat during our second Christmas, when I had made an emotional trip to Australia to see my mother for the first time in years.

It had been Bob who had really begun to slowly change my attitude to Christmas. Our first Christmas together, in 2007, was the simplest of affairs. The two of us had eaten a meal and then sat in front of the television for the day, but it was without doubt the happiest holiday season I'd ever had. It was the first time I'd got that Christmas 'feeling'.

By that point we'd been together for nine months and had been through a lot. When I'd found him he had looked like he'd been in a fight of some kind, probably with another animal. I'd assumed at first that he belonged to somebody else, but when I saw him rooted to the same spot a few days later I decided to do something about it. I'd taken him to see the local RSPCA where I'd bought some medication for him. I'd then gently nursed him back to health.

I'd taken an instant liking to him. He had a real personality, a quiet, knowing air. I'd tried to find his owners, but when no one claimed him I assumed he was a stray or street cat. That's when I'd named him Bob.

I'd expected our friendship to be a brief one. I guessed that he'd want to return to the streets once he was fit and well. He was a boisterous character and looked like he could handle himself out there. He had other ideas, however.

When I'd tried to send him on his way he refused to leave. To my amazement, one day he'd even jumped on board the bus I was travelling on so as to be with me.

And so it was that we had become inseparable. In many ways we were an odd couple but in others we were two peas in a pod, a pair of lost souls trying to survive day-to-day life in London. I also felt like he was my family. He provided the kindness and companionship and, yes, love that I'd craved for so long. He'd even given me the prospect of a new kind of life, one that just might get me off the streets. In the past few months I'd had a couple of unexpected encounters, the first with an

American lady who lived in Islington. She was a literary agent who had seen us sitting around Angel Tube station. She wondered whether the story of Bob and me might make a book. Subsequent to that, a few weeks ago, before the bad weather arrived, I'd met up with a writer who the agent thought might be able to help me get the story written. It was all very flattering, but I didn't expect it to amount to much – if anything at all. A book seemed a ridiculous pipe dream. That kind of success didn't happen to people like me.

I wasn't due to see the writer guy again until the New Year so I'd pretty much forgotten about it. It was a sign that perhaps things were turning around, that the future might just be brighter than it had

been for a very long time. In the short term, however, I knew it wasn't going to pay the gas and electric bills. The future wasn't a luxury I could afford to think about, I had to focus on surviving the present – and getting through this Christmas with Bob. I had a really bad feeling about what might lie ahead, and with good cause, as it turned out . . .

Chapter 3

Beep, beep, beep

Beep, beep, beep.

I woke up to the sound that I'd been dreading for days. It was Monday morning. The weekend was over and the £5 of emergency electricity we'd been living on had finally run out.

I knew that the beeping would repeat itself every minute for twenty minutes before falling silent. There were twelve beeps in each cycle and each one cut through me like a nagging headache. It was irritating, but there was nothing I could do about it unless I could get the card recharged. I jumped out of bed and rifled through my pockets. I had about £3.50 to my name, nowhere near enough to pay off the debt on the card. The situation was clear as day. That was it. We had no heating or lighting of any kind.

Beep, beep, beep. The meter went off again.

It was another grey, overcast morning and the house was bathed in shadow. The kitchen was quiet, with only the winking light of a battery-powered clock illuminating the gloom. I opened the fridge door and felt the contents. They were cold but wouldn't last for long.

I knew this moment had been coming. The meter wasn't going to continue to run on fresh air. But it was still a shock to the system. My mind was suddenly racing. How long could I leave the food before it would go off? How much money would I need in order to get the electric back on? How was I going to get both the gas and electricity running through the Christmas holidays? How were Bob and I going to cope if I simply couldn't raise the money? Would we have to head to a shelter or charity for Christmas? That particular thought was too awful to contemplate.

Beep, beep, beep.

There was a time, particularly when I was in the depths of my addiction, when I'd have panicked and been unable to cope with a setback like this. It was a measure of how much I'd changed that I almost immediately knew what to do.

It's strange how a crisis clarifies the mind. In a

way it simplified life for me. During the recent snow, I'd had a choice about going out. Now I had no such freedom. I had to get out there and earn enough money to get the electricity back on. Realistically, if I didn't do that within about nine hours, the Christmas stuff I had stored away would be ruined and would have to go in the dustbin. I simply couldn't allow that to happen.

I had a quick bowl of cereal, using the milk that was left in the fridge. I still had a reasonable supply of Bob's food, so I gave him a bowl of tuna and some water. I then went into a kind of autopilot mode and just started grabbing everything I needed to head out – my guitar, my copies of *The Big Issue*, my vendor's tabard. I threw in some more food for Bob and a roughly made sandwich for myself.

I looked outside. At least it wasn't snowing today. The rooftops still had a dusting of white powder on them, but there were cars moving around which meant that, with luck, there should also be some buses.

Beep, beep, beep.

As I headed out the door it felt a blessed relief to escape the sound, but I was soon experiencing another set of emotions. I headed off into the cold feeling a mixture of determination, uncertainty and slowly growing panic.

At the bus stop with Bob I made a plan of action.

I'd done some basic calculations. The bottom line was that I simply had to get the electric back on today. I had popped into the convenience store around the corner and got the balance checked. I needed to repay the £5 emergency loan and a further £6.50 for that to happen. So I needed a minimum of £11.50 to keep the contents of the fridge from going off.

I had also checked the gas card. I'd run up a debt of just under £15 on that. Realistically, I needed to put around £25 to £30 to get the heating and hot water back on and running for just a few days. This was the minimum target, but beyond that the next goal was to find a way of keeping the meter alive until this coming Thursday, December 23rd, the start of the Christmas holiday period. As long as I had some credit, even emergency credit, at 6 p.m. that evening, then I would be guaranteed to have energy through Christmas Eve, Christmas Day and Boxing Day. It would, however, go off again at 9 a.m. on December 27th.

I knew, however, that allowing that to happen really wasn't a good idea because the chances of me earning any money between Christmas and New Year were pretty slim. London was effectively a ghost town during that period. There was also the weather to take into account. What if we had more blizzards, as the Met Office were predicting? I'd be taking a big risk if I was going to rely on earning more money during that holiday week.

No, there was no doubt about it in my mind. My ultimate goal had to be to get myself through the next fortnight. I had to go all out to get enough money to stop worrying about the gas and electric until the New Year.

Of course, my energy bills weren't the only outgoings I had to contend with in the days ahead. I also had the rent on my flat, travel and Bob to take into account. So as we sat upstairs on the bus, heading into town, I scribbled a flurry of figures down on the back of an envelope. Taking everything into consideration, I had calculated that I needed to make another £150 in all. And I had to make that money in the next two to three days. It was going to be a very, very tall order. But I had to somehow find a way.

My first option was to step up my main source of income, selling *The Big Issue* at my pitch outside Angel Tube station in Islington. Very few people understood the way it worked. It wasn't a 'free' magazine that homeless people sold to make a few pounds. The charity had been set up to 'help people to help themselves' so vendors effectively ran their own businesses. We had to buy supplies of the magazine at a certain price and then sell them again at the cover price, making ourselves a profit – and hopefully a living – in the process.

This Christmas the magazine was selling for £2 and cost me £1 per copy, so I was making a clear £1 profit with each sale. As I weighed up my situation, I could see that I would have to sell dozens and dozens of magazines in the next few days. That simply wasn't going to happen.

Bob and I had built up a solid and loyal collection of supporters at Angel. Before we'd got there, I'd been reliably informed, our pitch outside the Tube station had been something of a graveyard for *The Big Issue* vendors. We'd made it a success. A lot of passers-by stopped to talk to us and lot of our customers bought the magazine off us week in, week out. But even allowing for that, I think the best I'd ever done in a single day was thirty magazines. The average was nearer fifteen to twenty. If I was going to save my Christmas, I needed to supplement this with other earnings. The most obvious was busking, which I knew was an option. Bob and I still did reasonably well singing in and around Covent Garden where, again, we had a core of people who gave us money on a regular basis. I would have to put in an extra shift doing that over the next couple of days. It wasn't a mission impossible, but it was going to be difficult, I knew that.

I wasn't being pessimistic, just realistic. I'd

worked on the streets for far too many Christmases so I knew very well that money was tight for everyone at this time of the year. And because money was so thin on the ground it was only natural that it became even more competitive between those who made a living busking, performing, begging or selling *The Big Issue*. The fact that there was a serious recession only added to the feeling that it was every man and woman for themselves. It really was survival of the fittest so I had to be fit over the next few days. Otherwise, my Christmas plans were not going to survive. If only it was that easy.

I arrived at Angel to discover the place was alive with activity, but not in a way that was good news for me. The concourse of the Tube station was packed with charity collectors, or 'chuggers' as many people refer to them because of the way they pester people often to the point of making them feel like they are being mugged. Of course, most of these collectors are working for legitimate charities like Greenpeace or Save the Children or Cancer Research who do important work, so I have never had an issue with those ones. They have as much right to be on the street as I do.

The problem is that there are an awful lot of other, less scrupulous 'charities' out there. A lot of them prey on young or vulnerable people and send them out to wave buckets in people's faces for hours on end, paying them a pittance. I'd seen groups of them moved on by the police in the past. On one occasion they did a spot check and found that the charity buckets weren't sealed as they were supposed to be in order to ensure the money goes directly to the charity. Another time, they'd found that the permits they were displaying had been cobbled together on Photoshop. They weren't licensed by the local authority or Transport for London who ran the Underground. They were just opportunists making money for themselves.

Needless to say, these collectors had no real concept of who else was working in the area and what the rules might be. And they had absolutely no concern for others who were trying to earn an honest crust.

I worked out pretty quickly that the people inside the Tube station today were from one of the more dubious charities. I'd never heard of them for a start. They claimed to be collecting for some vague Third World Anti-Poverty Fund. The badges they were carrying were bent and battered; it all looked pretty suspicious. There was nothing I could do about it as they seemed to have a licence to operate inside the station so all I could do was hope a community police officer or someone else would check them out and move them on if they were bogus. The lines were clearly drawn in that respect. I had a legitimate pitch outside the station, but I couldn't venture in there to sell my magazines. They were free to operate inside the Tube station.

The downside to this, from my point of view, was that the chuggers were getting to the commuters emerging from the Underground before me. It was bad news. And it wasn't long before it had become even worse.

As the evening wore on the chuggers and their buckets started to spill out on to the pavement outside as well. Before I knew it there was about half a dozen of them covering each of the exits, accosting everyone as they left.

I wasn't the only one who was annoyed by this. My pitch was opposite a flower stall and a newsagent. The owners of them were fuming at the way this mob were monopolising the area around the Tube entrance. Not only were they taking spare change that could have been diverted towards buying a magazine, a bunch of roses or a copy of *The Big Issue*, they were also driving people away. They were making people uncomfortable.

I watched as a long procession of commuters emerged from the Tube station with their heads bowed, unwilling to make eye contact with the chuggers, and by extension, anyone else. Any attempt I made to lift my voice above the noise of the buckets and the people wielding them was futile. I was just another voice. No one heard me.

Bob had been getting increasingly agitated. He could cope with almost all the noises London threw at him, but the sound of the buckets being shaken was making him nervous. He had curled up into a ball and had narrowed his eyes, a sure sign that he wasn't happy. At one point he hissed at a chugger who came too close. My sense of frustration was growing too. I'd managed to sell two copies of the magazine in almost an hour and a half. At that rate I wasn't going to earn enough to get home let alone to get the electric and gas running again.

I had been in this situation often enough to know that something was going to snap at some point, and sure enough it did.

I was in the process of selling a magazine to a regular customer when one of the chuggers started encroaching into my space. He was a big guy, about 6 ft tall and eighteen stone and was wearing a very bright, luminescent yellow bib. He had emerged out of the station and was backing towards me and Bob, shouting and waving his bucket around flamboyantly. He was getting closer and closer all the time

'Hey man, give us some space here,' I said, as politely as possible when he was within a couple of feet.

His response was less polite.

'What's your problem? I've got as much right to be here as you,' he said, holding his laminated permit in my face.

I gave him a dismissive look but told myself not to do anything silly.

I looked down and saw Bob was squeezed into a tiny space between my feet. He had effectively been driven into a corner; he looked so vulnerable. I was about to reach down to pick him up when the chugger lurched towards us and stuck his boot on the rucksack where Bob was sitting.

Eeeeew. Bob let out a loud screech.

'Oi, buddy, back off. You just stepped on my cat,' I said, leaning into the guy.

He just looked down at Bob and sneered.

'What's a bloody animal doing there in the first place?'

That was it, I was furious. I nudged him out of the way and he turned to face me. There was a bit of shouting but before it could get out of hand a community police officer appeared to separate us. I recognised him as he often patrolled the area.

'Come on, you two,' he said. 'What's the problem?'

To be fair to the policeman, he understood. He asked the guy to stick to his designated area, which he did, much to his displeasure. He was a pretty unpleasant-looking character and kept glaring at me from the concourse. I sensed that he might cause more trouble once the policeman had left, so I made a decision; this was no place for Bob, we needed to head off elsewhere. I gathered my stuff together and slipped into the Tube station via another one of the entrances. By the time the guy noticed us we had gone through the ticket barriers and were on the escalator heading down.

I decided to head to Covent Garden where I might be able to buy a few more magazines or, failing that, do an hour or two of busking. There was no point in heading home yet. For all I knew, the weather might get even worse than this and I might be trapped indoors for a month. I had to make the most of my opportunities.

We took the Tube, mainly just to keep warm. Bob drew lots of admiring glances, as usual, but there were the inevitable sneers and snide remarks as well.

'What are you doing to the poor creature?' one elderly lady said to me.

'He's fine, madam, don't worry about him,' I said, but it didn't placate her and she started lecturing me.

I'd had this argument a thousand times. Bob had chosen me, rather than the other way around. He could leave me at any time, he had ample opportunity. But he didn't, he preferred to be at my side. It was his choice. On this occasion, however, I was simply too tired and cold and anxious about Christmas to be bothered. I simply hopped off the Tube at the next stop, walked down the platform and got back on again, this time in another, quieter carriage where, thankfully, we were left in peace.

I didn't want to get into trouble with *The Big Issue* for selling the magazine away from my authorised pitch, so I had planned to talk to Sam, the regular *Big Issue* co-ordinator at Covent Garden to make sure it was all right. Unfortunately she was nowhere to be seen, so I had no option but to get my guitar out and do a little busking. I found a spot near the end of James Street, off the Piazza, where I'd played for many years.

It was never easy busking in the freezing cold. The cold could have a detrimental effect on the guitar, warping the neck so that it needed constant tuning. Sometimes it got so cold the strings would snap. As I started strumming away, however, the biggest problem was my fingers. I was wearing a pair of black fingerless gloves that a regular customer at Angel had given me. She had noticed me rubbing my hands all the time and dashed off to buy them for me. But even the gloves couldn't protect my fingers from the effects of the cold. My fingers burned when I played the metal strings. It didn't sound great either. It all felt a bit half-hearted.

As if that wasn't bad enough, people could barely hear me. The area was crammed full of street performers. It was a cacophony of noise, with buskers, clowns and even the living statues vying to make themselves heard above the din. The noise was simply too much; I'd have needed an amplifier to make my presence felt.

I decided to head away from here, down Neal Street. It was quieter, but at least there was a chance we could be heard there.

As I set up once more, I went through my pockets and took stock of how the day was going. It wasn't good news. I had been out for the best part of five hours but had barely earned £10. It was depressing.

Neal Street was little better.

There was a very strange atmosphere. A couple of shops were really busy. In particular, a trendy store selling classic American-style parkas was thronged with youngsters, tourists probably, who hadn't bargained on this weather and were seemingly buying some fashionable winter-wear. On Monmouth Street, the famous coffee shop had queues snaking down the road. But a lot of the other shops, bars and restaurants were closed. Parts of the street were deserted. It was a bit surreal.

We set ourselves up near the shop selling the parkas. A few passers-by stopped to say hello to

Bob and take a picture. He had always been photo-genic. I'd soon accumulated a few coins but it was clear this was going to be a poor day.

For a moment my mind drifted back to the time, during my very early days with Bob, when a guy had casually dropped £200 into my hands. It had come completely out of the blue. The guy hadn't even looked wealthy. He was in a leather jacket and jeans. He'd just rolled out a few notes and dropped them into the top pocket of my jacket with a cursory 'There you go, man.' I'd assumed it was a couple of fivers, but it turned out to be four £50 notes. I'd been completely shocked and had looked for the guy, but he'd disappeared into the crowds. My guess is that he was some kind of musician or maybe an actor. Perhaps I should have recognised him, but I hadn't.

'Oh, for a £200 drop today, eh, Bob?' I said.

A boy could dream.

The wind had a habit of whipping its way down Neal Street and by late afternoon it was clear Bob had had enough of sitting in the cold.

'Come on, mate, let's call it quits for the day,' I said.

We were in the process of packing up when I heard a voice.

'James, wait. Wait.'

Running towards us was a middle-aged lady,

Jane, who had been supporting us for years. She was a little breathless.

'Oh, I've been looking for you two everywhere. I'm so glad I've found you.'

She handed me a smart-looking bag. It took me a while to work out what it was. Inside was a bright red hat with a bell on top and a small red jacket with white trimming.

'Oh wow, it's a Santa Paws outfit for Bob,' I said.

'I saw it in a shop the other day and couldn't resist.'

Belle had made Bob an outfit similar to this a few years ago. She'd rustled it up herself on a sewing machine, but it was long lost. This new one was really good quality; Jane must have spent a lot of money on it.

I felt awful. Part of me was grateful that someone had taken the trouble to get such a thoughtful present. But another part of me was wondering how precisely this was going to help me heat my flat and feed Bob and I through the Christmas holidays.

She stayed and chatted to us for a while then gave me a Christmas card.

'If you need anything let me know,' she said. 'My phone number's inside the card.'

I was too embarrassed to tell her that I hadn't topped up my battered old mobile phone in a fortnight and was highly unlikely to do so again for a while.

As Jane headed off back towards Covent Garden I opened the card. To my delight I found £10 inside the Christmas card. I immediately, felt guilty for thinking such ungrateful thoughts earlier. I felt like heading back to Covent Garden and looking for Jane to say thank you, but I knew she'd be long gone.

We headed back to Tottenham Court Road via Seven Dials. There was no mistaking the fact that Christmas was almost upon us. I watched a line of families filing into the theatre on the corner, some with little babies in their arms. It took me back to my only experience of a pantomime at Christmas.

A school choir was singing on another corner, a small crowd of parents and friends encouraging them as they performed in the bitterly cold evening. I recognised the melody of the carol they were singing immediately; it was 'Good King Wenceslas'.

I couldn't help shaking my head at the irony. The words told the story of a kindly old king helping a 'poor man' he took pity on as he was 'gath'ring winter's fuel'.

'Hmm, that sounds familiar, Bob,' I said, ruffling Bob's head and moving on towards Tottenham Court Road.

In some ways the words of the carol should have been reassuring. I wasn't the first, nor would I be the last person to find themselves struggling at Christmas. But I found it hard to find solace.

On the bus I totted up what I had earned today. Including Jane's generous last-minute gift I had just over £25. It was enough to get my electricity back on and allow me to buy some milk, bread and a few other bits and pieces in the local corner shop, but no more. The gas – and my first warm shower in a week – would have to wait until another day. I'd survived on cold ones until now. Another one wouldn't kill me.

I limped home feeling deflated, frustrated and a little alarmed at what the next week or so had in store for us. That long-term target of £150 seemed a distant prospect. I feared that I was going to

spend my Christmas on tenterhooks, dashing back and forth to the corner shop to heat up the flat whenever I managed to earn a few quid.

The temperature seemed to be dropping on a daily basis. As the wind cut through us, I felt Bob wrapping himself tighter and tighter around my neck so that his head was almost buried in the collar of my coat.

'Sorry, Bob, but I think you are going to have to get used to this. It's going to be a long, cold Christmas,' I said as we arrived back in the still chilly flat.

We spent the evening on the sofa together, keeping each other warm under not just one but two blankets.

Chapter 4

Miracle on Upper Street

Bob's intelligence never ceases to amaze me, not least when it comes to devising ways to wake me up in the morning.

I can be a heavy sleeper; there are times when a bomb could go off around me and I wouldn't stir. So Bob has become the master of finding ingenious ways to rouse me from my slumbers.

One of his techniques involves putting his front paws on the mattress so that he is looking directly into my eyes and making loud *waaauuwahhh* noises as he looks up at me. I can't prove this for certain, but I'm pretty sure that on a couple of occasions he used another method in which he threw his favourite toy, a scraggedy mouse, on to my pillow.

I'd woken up to find it an inch or so from my nose. There was no other explanation for it being there.

Today, however, he had resorted to yet another method and had slid alongside me, placing his head next to mine where he had begun purring loudly in my ear. I must have been in a pretty deep sleep, because when I began to come out of it I found it hard to work out what the sound was. It was so intense that for one bizarre moment I thought there was a workman with a pneumatic drill in the hallway outside. It made me sit bolt upright in my bed.

I could never be cross with him for doing this. How could I? The fact that his handsome face was the first thing I saw each morning was a blessing. Even if, like today, it was wearing an expression that said, *Come on, lazy bones. I should have had my breakfast half an hour ago.*

After topping up the electric the previous night, I had awarded myself a much-appreciated lie in. It was such a relief not to wake up instinctively around 9 a.m. and lie there waiting in silence for the meter to decide my fate.

It was well past 10 a.m. when I finally got up. As I slid out of bed the cold was a shock to the system. It must have been well below zero. As I walked into the living room, I half expected to see icicles forming on the ceiling. I stood shivering in the kitchen while I made Bob his breakfast and boiled the kettle for a reviving cup of tea. I was still determined to go out again today. Yesterday had been tough, but I simply didn't have the option of letting it get me down.

I flicked the television on and immediately wished I hadn't. A news bulletin was giving out a weather forecast. It wasn't good news. The map was covered in snowflake symbols; there was more snow on the way.

'Brilliant,' I sighed to myself. 'Just what I needed.'

Unfortunately I knew there was no alternative. I had to get out there again, even if only for a few hours.

As usual, I gave Bob the option of staying at home. He'd exercised his right to stay in the flat a couple of times in the past weeks, which was fine. There was no question that I did better when he was around. Without him I became another invisible street-person. But I'd always understood that I wasn't his master. No human 'owned' a cat. He was free to do as he pleased so when he remained lying by the radiator or more recently on the sofa, I respected his wishes and left him alone. Today, however, he headed for the door as soon as he saw me gathering my guitar and rucksack together.

'OK, mate, going to be a cold one again today, apparently,' I said.

I grabbed the Santa Paws outfit and helped him into it. It looked really cute, I had to admit, and it had the advantage of providing him with an extra layer, which made it doubly effective. I also packed one of his thickest scarves for good measure.

The sky was the colour of charcoal and there was a sub-zero wind blowing straight at us as we walked down the still icy street towards the bus stop.

The bus was pretty empty so we managed to get our favourite spot, at the front of the upper deck. Bob loves sitting there, watching the world go by. I was more concerned with the weather and kept looking up at the scarily dark skies. I was no meteorologist, but it was pretty obvious that the weather was worsening and that something nasty was on its way. I'd been hoping that the snow would arrive later in the day, preferably that night, but I had a feeling it was a lot closer than that. My instincts were soon proven right.

We were halfway through our journey and approaching the Essex Road railway station when the first flakes of snow appeared. The transformation was amazing to behold. Suddenly the world looked like the inside of one of those Christmas ornaments filled with desiccated coconut that you shake to create a snowstorm. One moment I could see clearly out of the upper-deck window. The next the glass was a sheet of off-white snow and I couldn't see a thing.

It didn't take long for the traffic to grind to a halt and within minutes the bus had stopped. Through the side window I could see that cars were sliding all over the road and it soon became apparent there had been an accident ahead. The bus driver made an apologetic announcement that we would have to wait for the accident to be sorted out.

I took an executive decision.

'Come on, Bob, we'll walk the last bit.'

In anticipation of the snow, I had packed a plastic bag with a hole for his head. I'd done something similar before, when the first snows had arrived a month or so ago, where I'd improvised a plastic bag I'd bought in a newsagent. It had worked pretty well so I'd got into the habit of carrying a supermarket plastic bag with me at all times, just in case. I slipped him into this latest makeshift poncho and got off the bus.

It would normally have been a twenty-minute walk or so to Angel, but the snow was so heavy it was going to take double that I reckoned. We'd need to stop a couple of times just to get some warmth. There were a couple of places I knew where, unlike most other, they were happy for me to come in with Bob.

That was the plan in any case. It didn't take long for it to unravel.

The snow was still falling heavily and was settling on top of the hard, impacted stuff that had been there for the past week or so. This was making it really difficult to walk on again, especially as Bob was restless to get down all the time. He loved walking in the snow and was eager to have a run around.

'No, Bob, stay there, mate,' I said a couple of times, placing a hand on his back to hold him in position.

He wasn't very happy about it, but he got the message.

I'd just done this again when I was distracted by some kids having a snowball fight. They were innocent enough but I just didn't want them to throw one at me with Bob on my shoulder. It proved my undoing.

I was so focussed on where the kids were aiming their snowballs that I didn't look where I was about to step. There was a section of black ice ahead of me. The moment my boot hit it my legs went from underneath me.

'*Whooooah.*'

'*Eeeeeew.*'

We both shouted.

Fortunately, Bob, being a cat, was able to

self-right himself and landed safely on his feet. I wasn't so lucky. I landed badly on my backside and it really hurt.

I lay on the snow in agony for what felt like a couple of minutes, groaning. Bob was instantly at my side. At first he looked at me as if weighing up the situation.

'What have you done now?' his expression seemed to be saying.

But he soon worked out that I was in genuine pain. He began sniffing around me and putting his paw on my leg, as if knowing it was in pain, which it was.

As I took stock of what had happened I realised that I had actually been lucky. Fortunately I had my guitar and rucksack on my back and they had protected my head as it snapped back. If they hadn't been there I might have been in real trouble. I could have knocked myself out – or even worse.

That was the good news. The bad news was that the guitar hit the ground really hard.

I had a sinking feeling immediately.

I got myself up and headed into the doorway of an office building where I dropped to my knees and opened the guitar case. It confirmed my worst fears. The guitar went back to the days when I was in the band Hyper Fury in around 2002. I had bought it from a Spanish guy I knew called Picha for £50. It was a black, steel-string acoustic Kimbara with red edging. It was already fairly battered and bruised. During my time busking it had taken knocks and dents on the buses and on the Tube as people bashed into it. I'd even had to tape it up a few times. The damage this time, however, looked more serious than anything that had happened before. Because of the way I had fallen, the bottom of the guitar had taken the full force of the impact and the front panel had loosened.

It was now totally unplayable.

I felt sick. I was in a desperate situation and my guitar was one of the two things that could get me out of it. Now it was broken! What the hell was I going to do? What was life going to throw at me next?

Bob had always been incredibly well tuned to my moods and immediately picked up on the fact I was distressed. As I sat in the doorway, he hopped on to my lap and stuck his head into the space under my chin, rubbing my neck and purring gently. It was as if he was saying, *'Don't worry, mate, we will be OK*. He had an amazing knack for making me feel better. I sat there for a few minutes, trying to gather my thoughts – and my strength.

'OK, you're right, mate. I'm still standing. Let's get going,' I said after a while.

I had no option. I had to press on.

Thankfully the snow eased a little bit for the next few minutes and I was able to hobble along to Angel. My mood didn't improve much when we arrived at our pitch. After taking Bob's poncho off, I set myself up. I looked through my pockets. I pulled out my Oyster travel card and saw that it had also been damaged in the fall. It was bent in half and almost broken. There was no way it would be accepted at Tube stations or on buses in that state. It was another setback.

One of the first people I saw was a guy who often stopped for a chat, Paul. He bought a *Big Issue* then gave me a fiver. He was with another guy, a big, thickset brute of a man with a shaved head and a tattoo on his neck.

He immediately started having a go at Paul.

'What did you do that for?' he said.

'What?' Paul said.

'Why did you give him a bloody fiver? Look at him, he's only gonna go and blow it all on smack or crack or some other crap.'

'No he's not,' he said. 'He's just trying to get his life back together. Give the guy a break.'

For a moment I thought they were going to come to blows. Reluctantly, I readied myself to intervene. Fortunately, a community police officer was hovering again and made his presence felt. They soon moved along.

The two continued their argument down the road, both of them shouting and waving their arms as they went. It made me sad, but it didn't surprise me. It summed up the attitude I'd faced ever since I'd started working on the streets. Some people were willing to give me the benefit of the doubt and try to help. Others weren't. It was as simple as that.

By now it was mid-afternoon. The long bus journey and my accident had wasted a lot of time. I knew we couldn't stay for long. It was simply too cold. Fortunately Bob's new Santa Paws outfit had immediately drawn attention.

'Oh look, that's so cuuuuute,' one American tourist said, setting the trend for the next couple of hours. I must have heard that phrase fifty times by the end of the afternoon. People simply couldn't resist stopping and taking a photograph. To my delight, most of them bought magazines. It cheered me up a little.

By late afternoon, as the number of people passing through the station began to build, business was really flourishing. I'd already had to run over to the *Big Issue* co-ordinator's stand and top up my supply of magazines. I'd had a good feeling about the way things were going and reinvested most of my money. It was a gamble, but I felt it was one worth taking.

Bob had always had an uncanny knack of

knowing when I really needed him to turn on the charm and he seemed to sense it today. We had a few tricks that we did which seemed to please the crowds. I would use treats to get him to stand on his hind legs. He would sometimes grab my arms so that I lifted him off the ground in this position. This afternoon he seemed to be initiating all the play. It was as if he had sensed our opportunity and was saying, *Come on, mate, let's make hay while the sun shines*. Not that the sun was shining, of course. The weather was still grim although, thankfully, the snow had abated now.

I knew we were doing well but I also remembered the golden rules of being on the street. I was sure to put all the money I'd made inside a purse which I'd put deep inside my coat. I couldn't be too careful. I'd been the victim of pickpockets and threatening thugs here before. I simply couldn't afford to have that happen again today. It would have been too much to bear.

The day had already been an eventful one. It had begun disastrously but had begun to improve a little. It was about to get a lot, lot better, however.

It was around 4.30 p.m., just after dark at this time of year, that something interesting began to happen. We hadn't spent much time here outside the Tube station for almost a fortnight now. When we had made an appearance, we'd either been driven away by the weather or the seemingly ever-present chuggers who made life so difficult for us. Today, however, there was no sign of any of them. It felt great to have the place to ourselves again, especially as people seemed so genuinely pleased to see us.

The first inkling I got about how much people had been missing us came when two friends from the Tube station appeared, Davika and Amy.

'Hello, you two, where have you been hiding? Somewhere warm I hope,' Davika said.

I didn't have the heart to tell her we were living in an igloo.

I explained what had happened earlier and showed them my rather sad-looking guitar.

'Hold on a minute,' Amy said, disappearing inside the station.

She soon reappeared with a large roll of gaffer tape.

Between us we had soon fixed the front panel. The rear of the body of the guitar was now wrapped in about ten layers of thick tape, but I didn't care. It made a reasonable sound again, so I could go busking later if necessary.

As it turned out, it wasn't necessary. Quite the opposite. We didn't need to go anywhere.

As the rush hour began to build we began to see a lot of our regular commuter customers making their way home from work. One of the first was a lady called Angela, one of our most loyal supporters. I saw her approaching from a distance. She'd been walking along with her head down, looking a little bit down in the dumps but had then spotted us. Her body language had immediately changed and she'd almost broken into a jog, which was quite impressive given that she must have been well into her seventies.

'Oh, what a lovely surprise. I didn't think we'd see you again before Christmas, what with this awful weather,' she said, excitedly.

'No, we will be here now for a few days,' I said. 'Need to earn some money to get us through the holidays, you know?'

'Ah, yes,' Angela said, suddenly digging around in her handbag. 'Oh where is it? I've been carrying this around for a fortnight, hoping to see you. Aaah, here we go,' she said, producing a white envelope.

It was a Christmas card.

'Oh, thanks a lot,' I said, immediately feeling guilty again that I didn't have one for her.

'I put in a little something to help you through Christmas. I know it's a hard time of the year.'

'Angela, that's really thoughtful.'

I was dying to open it, but fought the urge to do so in front of her. She kneeled down and stroked

Bob for a while as we chatted. She stayed with us for at least ten minutes.

My curiosity got the better of me almost as soon as she walked away. I opened the envelope and saw there was £40 in there. I felt a strange mix of gratitude and relief. I couldn't quite believe that someone had been so generous.

'Up we go, Bob,' I said, treating him to a snack, a broad smile on my face. He stood on his hind legs immediately, drawing the usual *ooohs* and *aaaahs* from the thickening crowd outside the Tube station. There was even a flurry of flashes from people's camera phones. We had often created this kind of atmosphere during the summer but it was rare at this time of the year. It felt good to be back in the limelight. It felt good to be making some money too.

I'd barely put the money from Angela safely inside my coat when another regular visitor appeared.

'Aha, the dynamic duo. You've ventured out to see us before Christmas,' she said.

She too produced a card. 'Nothing much, but I just wanted to show you that I am thinking of you at this time of the year.'

By now I was feeling quite emotional about this seemingly spontaneous outpouring of kindness.

'Gosh, everyone is so kind. I can't believe how

many people are giving me cards today,' I said to the lady after seeing that her card contained another £10.

'That's what Christmas is all about, isn't it?' she said. 'Showing kindness to each other, especially those who are less fortunate than us.'

In the space of the next two hours I received another half-dozen cards. One contained a voucher for Marks & Spencer, which was lovely. I'd never have been able to afford their food in ordinary circumstances. Three of the others contained money. Every time I opened a card and found a fiver or a tenner inside, my spirits soared. But it wasn't just the money that touched me; some of the messages inside the cards almost reduced me to tears.

It was soon clear that a lot of people had been planning on giving us cards in our absence. By early evening I reckoned I'd accumulated close to £100. I was ecstatic. It felt like a minor miracle. And it hadn't happened on 34th Street, or wherever that Hollywood movie about Father Christmas had been set. It had happened here on Upper Street.

All the worries of earlier in the day suddenly dissipated. I'd even forgotten about the throbbing pain from my fall. My mind was already flying ahead in time, wondering what delicious treat I was going to buy in Marks & Spencer when I spent the voucher.

'Isn't life strange,' I said to myself. 'Twenty-four hours ago I was convinced we'd have to check into a shelter or go to a food bank for Christmas dinner. Now I'm fantasising over sticky toffee pudding.'

I didn't want to keep Bob out in the cold any longer than necessary, but I hung around for an extra half an hour so that regulars who tended to arrive home from work a little later could see us. It was crazy really, but a small part of me now felt guilty that I'd denied people the chance to wish us both a Merry Christmas. It was clear that a lot of people had been disappointed not to see us lately. I didn't want to disappoint them again.

Sure enough, a handful of others came over, as delighted as everyone else to see that we were alive and well.

'Someone told me you'd moved away from London,' one guy said.

Another lady said she'd heard I was very ill. It felt like some kind of homecoming. We were being welcomed like returning heroes, almost. The temperature was approaching zero again, but it warmed the cockles of my heart.

Bob and I eventually got away about 7.30 p.m.

So much had happened that I'd forgotten about my disfigured Oyster card. As I climbed on the bus

I tried to shape it back into some semblance of normality but almost succeeded in snapping it in half.

Some bus drivers wouldn't have allowed me to travel with the card in that state, but fortunately the driver this evening was a decent soul.

'Give it here,' he said, when I tried unsuccessfully to scan the card on the reader.

After a few moments manipulating the card carefully, he got it straight again. To my amazement it made the usual ping sound when he ran it along the reader.

'There you go,' he said with a smile.

'Cheers, mate, you're a saviour,' I said.

The bus journey was slow again, but I didn't care. My mind was working overtime as all sorts of thoughts raced through my head. I felt elated. But I also felt touched beyond belief. I'd known we were popular at Angel, but I didn't realise that we were held in quite such deep affection. There was no other way of putting it: we were loved. And that made me feel quite emotional.

I also felt incredibly blessed.

As I looked out at the rows of houses with their bright Christmas decorations lit up in the windows, I realised how lucky I was. Yes, I'd had a rough life and suffered a lot of setbacks, many of them self-inflicted. But throughout, one thing had been consistent. I'd been the beneficiary of so much kindness, often from completely random people, from care workers to drug counsellors, outreach workers to ordinary people who took the time to talk to me when I was on the street. London had such a bad reputation but its streets were filled with good souls. The man driving my bus at this precise moment was another. There were so many of them. On their own, their acts of kindness didn't amount to much. Taken together, they had probably saved my life.

What had happened today outside Angel was a prime example of this. I thought about all those people coming up to me and giving me cards and money. None of them needed to do it. They'd done so out of the goodness of their hearts, they'd done so in the spirit of Christmas. That mysterious, magical thing that had previously eluded me. I was so grateful.

That gave way to another thought, however. I felt bad that I'd not really shown my gratitude properly. Not just today, not ever. When I was younger that had been a little more understandable. I hadn't been in a fit state to do so. I was usually either too angry or too high to even say a proper thank you. But that was another time, almost another me. I was a different person now. Now I had no excuse, now I could say thank you. And it was the perfect time of the year to do so. As

I sat there on the bus, I made a resolution. I had an opportunity and I was going to take it. It felt like a small epiphany.

On the way back to the flat I called in at the convenience store and topped up both the electricity and the gas. I put £80 on, £40 on each. It was enough to get me through Christmas and beyond, I felt sure. I couldn't help shaking my head at the changes that had come over me. A few years ago there would have been no way I'd have done anything as sensible as this. I'd have blown that money on drugs. But now I had a different perspective on life. I also had someone else to care for.

Bob was standing patiently on my shoulder, but I could tell he was tired and cold. I was looking forward to warming the flat up so that he could thoroughly thaw out by the radiator.

I picked up a pint of milk and a snack for Bob and put them on the counter.

'Is that all?' the guy next to the till asked.

'Oh. No, hold on,' I said, suddenly remembering the resolution I'd made on the bus.

I headed over to the small stationery section in the store. It didn't have a great selection of Christmas cards. I guessed that most people had bought their cards weeks ago. Eventually, however, I found a stack of boxed collections of cards, each with simple seasonal messages on them. There were six boxes in the stack, each containing a dozen cards. I took two.

'You have a lot of friends,' the guy behind the counter said as he rang the boxes up on the till.

It was an innocent enough comment, he was only trying to make polite conversation, but it made me think.

'Actually, you're right. I do,' I said smiling.

I ran over to the stack of Christmas cards and grabbed the other four boxes.

'I'll take these as well,' I said.

Chapter 5

Smiley Faces

The Arctic weather was making all the news again. When I flicked the television on the next morning, the breakfast bulletin was claiming it was the coldest winter in exactly a century, since 1910. The programme was full of dramatic stories of people's troubles in the past twenty-four hours. Cars and lorries had been trapped in giant snowdrifts, flights had been cancelled, shopping centres and motor-ways were being forced to close. According to one bulletin from Heathrow, there had been fist fights as distraught travellers realised they were stranded in London, possibly over the Christmas holiday. Someone called it the Christmas from hell. A day ago, I could have related to that. Yesterday, however, had been a heavenly release from my worries.

I wasn't entirely out of the woods. I wanted to get Belle and Bob some half-decent presents and needed a little bit of spare cash to cover contingencies during the holiday. I also wanted to top up my phone so that I could try to call my dad on Christmas Day. Most of all, however, I wanted to get to Angel today. I had something I needed to do.

I gave Bob his breakfast and made myself a bowl of hot cereal.

'Central heating for kids, the adverts call it. Let's see if it works for thirty-one-year-old kids, shall we, Bob?' I said, as I spooned the bowl down.

The television was still broadcasting weather news. When one of the meteorologists began predicting even more atrocious weather with lots of temperatures below minus ten degrees centigrade later this week, I decided I'd heard enough.

'Let's go, Bob. The sooner we get out there, the sooner we get home again.'

The landscape was still as white as it had been yesterday, but at least London seemed to be moving again. The roads had been cleared pretty well so the bus journey was a million times better than the previous day.

When we got to Angel, I laid out our pitch as

normal, with one exception. I had four boxes of Christmas cards with me. I had spent the previous night writing messages in about half of them. I'd gone to bed with a sore arm to go with my sore backside. The rest remained blank, although it didn't take long for that to change.

As had happened yesterday, a lot of people reacted to us as if they were being reunited with long-lost relatives.

'Ah, that's cheered me up seeing you two back,' said one regular, a young girl called Bernadette who worked in some offices not far from the Tube station.

As she kneeled down to stroke Bob, I took a blank card out of one of the boxes and started scribbling:

To Bernadette, have a great Xmas, luv James and Bob.

I then drew a heart shape under my name and a smiley face with whiskers and pointy cat's ears under Bob's. She seemed genuinely touched when I gave it to her.

'Oh that's absolutely lovely,' she said, holding her hand to her face as if she was going to shed a tear.

'I do love seeing you two, you know. It really

does make my day. Especially when I've had a belly full of that lot in there,' she said, pointing at her office block.

'It's our pleasure, honestly,' I said. 'Have a great Christmas.'

'You too,' she said.

As I watched her walk off I kneeled down and gave Bob an affectionate stroke.

'There goes one happy customer, mate,' I said. 'Let's see how many more smiles we can put on people's faces today.'

I had decided that I was going to give a card to everyone who bought a *Big Issue* today, regardless of whether they were a regular customer or not. I had two boxes of blank ones to make out personally to regulars whose names I knew. The other two boxes contained the ready-signed ones that I would give to everyone else we saw today.

One or two people looked a bit perplexed at being handed a Christmas card by a *Big Issue* vendor. One young guy who bought the magazine off me looked at it as if he'd been given a letter sacking him from his job. I was pretty sure that he would dispose of it in the first dustbin he found. I didn't mind. I'd made the gesture and that was more than enough for me.

A few people came along having seen me the previous day with cards of their own.

'I saw you here last night but didn't have this with me,' one regular, Mary, said, producing a large blue envelope with James and Bobby written on the cover. I had no idea why she had renamed him, but I didn't mind.

'Thanks, Mary,' I said. 'Talk to Bob, er, I mean Bobby, for a second will you, I've got something for you.'

Her face lit up when she saw the personalised message.

'Now that is getting pride of place on my mantelpiece this Christmas,' she said.

Another lady, a rather quiet and timid soul who often stopped just to admire Bob, arrived clutching not just a card but a little present as well.

'It's just a little catnip mouse for Bob,' she said.

'Oh, that's very kind of you, he will enjoy that,' I said.

She seemed chattier than normal and stopped for a couple of minutes.

'So what are you two doing for Christmas?' she asked.

'Nothing much, just the two of us in front of the telly eating something nice, I hope.'

'Sounds lovely,' she said.

'Not much compared to the big day that other people have.'

'Yes, but you will probably be a lot more content

than a lot of those people. You are spending the day with someone who makes you happy and who won't argue with you, so I've got a feeling there will probably be more love in your living room than theirs.'

It caught me off guard a little. I'd never thought of us in those terms, but it set me thinking. When I looked at all the people rushing past us each day, I often wondered what sort of lives they led, what sort of homes they were heading back to each evening. To judge by the expression on some of their faces, I felt sure a lot of them were leading pretty empty, unhappy existences. They looked completely stressed out. She was probably right. Their homes might be bigger and contain a lot more material possessions than mine. That wouldn't be difficult, I had next to nothing. Yet since I'd found Bob my home had always been full of that precious commodity that, as a certain foursome once sang, money can't buy you. Love. It was a lovely thought, one that stayed with me for most of the day.

I had brought fifty cards with me. I was soon panicking that it wasn't enough. Nothing could detract from the happiness I was feeling, however. The amount of money I was earning had suddenly become a minor consideration. I was having a great time handing out cards, enjoying people's reactions. I was too busy having a good time to analyse what it all meant. Someone else did that for me, as it turned out.

As the afternoon turned into early evening I was aware of a guy handing out leaflets near me. He was smartly dressed, in a grey suit and a dark blue tie. He wasn't pushy or noisy. In fact he seemed a very gentle soul. He would quietly extend his hand in front of people as they approached then nod and mouth 'Thank you' if they acknowledged him. One or two people had engaged him in a chat. It all seemed very friendly, which was a pleasant change, especially after my confrontation with the chugger a couple of nights earlier. We'd exchanged glances a couple of times during the first hour or so he'd been there.

It was coming up to the busiest time of the day, rush hour, but, in a lull in activity around the Tube station, he came over.

'My, that's a lovely cat you have there, my friend,' he said. 'Hope you don't mind me coming over and saying hello to him. What's his name?'

'Bob.'

'Bob,' he said, dropping to his knees. 'Would Bob mind if I stroked him?'

'No, go ahead, just make sure you stroke him on the back of the neck.'

'Sure,' he said.

He had an accent I couldn't quite place. There were hints of American in it, but there was something else there as well.

I was writing out a few more Christmas cards so wasn't in the chattiest of moods. But he was harmless enough so, more out of politeness than anything, I thought I'd better engage.

'So what are the leaflets you are handing out?' I said.

'Oh, it's an invitation to a church service I'm speaking at on Christmas Eve,' he replied, handing me one of his flyers.

I recoiled immediately. I'd been raised in a strong Christian environment and had had some very bad experiences. I hadn't rejected it as a religion, but I had distanced myself ever since. If pushed about my faith these days, I always said I was a Buddhist, which was kind of true. I'd read a lot of stuff by the Dalai Lama and found great wisdom and support in it, especially through some of the darker times in my life.

'No thanks, mate, I don't really do Christianity,' I said, perhaps a little too sharply.

I saw a quizzical look flash across his face. I could tell he was trying to work me out.

'Not a problem, my friend,' he said, standing up.

'I'll let you carry on with your Christmas cards. Thanks for letting me say hello to Bob.'

I felt a little bit guilty. I hadn't meant to be rude but equally I didn't want to get reeled into a conversation on religion. Even at Christmas.

I soon forgot about him. Almost immediately, one of my regular customers appeared.

'Oh, hello, Jeremy,' I said, recognising him. 'I've got something for you.'

He too seemed genuinely pleased when I gave him a card. He opened it up and chuckled warmly when he saw the smiley-face Bob signature.

'I'm sorry, James, I've got no cash on me at the moment,' he said, slightly embarrassed.

'Don't worry about it. You've been really generous through the year. I just wanted to give you a card to say thanks,' I said.

'Oh, OK. Well Happy Christmas to the pair of you. I really hope you have a peaceful time.'

In the space of the next half an hour, I had similar exchanges with about half a dozen familiar faces. I knew some of them by name, but others were just recognisable faces that, I knew, had bought the magazine off me at some point in the past. I gave each of them a card. Some had bought a magazine off me, but others, like Jeremy, hadn't. I'd made sure to reassure each of them that it wasn't a problem.

The rush hour actually felt more like a rush half-hour this evening. I got the feeling that a lot of people had already finished work for the Christmas holidays and were wrapped up warm at home. Lucky so-and-sos.

I'd been so tied up in talking to people that I hadn't paid attention to the guy from the church earlier. I assumed he'd left. When I looked around, however, I saw that he was still there. He was now occupying a spot behind me. He only seemed to have a few flyers left.

My conscience was still nagging me about the way I spoke to him earlier, so I got Bob to jump on my shoulder and headed over towards him, a card in my hand.

'Here you go, mate,' I said, walking over to him. 'I hope I didn't offend you earlier. Happy Christmas.'

He accepted the card with a smile. He laughed out loud when he saw the smiley face.

'Wonderful,' he said.

There was a real lull in activity now, so I took the opportunity to light up a cigarette.

'Smoke?' I said, offering the guy my packet.

'No thanks.'

'So where are you from?'

'London, via South Africa and New York,' he said. 'It's complicated.'

'Life is,' I smiled.

'Indeed.'

'So what's your sermon about on Christmas Eve?' I said, drawing on my cigarette.

'Messages the Bible can teach us at this time of the year. You know, the usual stuff.'

'No, I don't know,' I said. 'I had a bad time with Christianity when I was little.'

'Really?' he said. 'You don't behave that way.'

'What do you mean?'

'There's something very Christian, with a small c, about the way you behave.'

I could feel myself bridling again at the prospect of getting into a religious discussion, but I didn't want to appear rude a second time.

'In what way exactly?' I said.

'Oh, as in Acts 32, verse 5,' he smiled, as if testing me.

'Go on, you've got me,' I said. 'What does it say in verse 5 of Acts, thirty-something?'

He looked at me for a moment, again weighing me up. He then recited what I assumed was a direct passage from the Bible.

' "In all things I have shown you that by working hard in this way we must help the weak and remember the words of the Lord Jesus, how he himself said, 'It is more blessed to give than to receive.' "'

I shook my head. I didn't quite get it.

'I overheard you talking to some of the people

who came up to you. I could see how happy you were giving to them rather than just having to rely on their charity.'

'And . . .?'

'And I thought to myself "there's someone who has learned that it is more blessed to give than to receive".'

I just smiled at him. I wasn't sure what to say.

There was an awkward silence for a moment.

'Anyhow, I have got rid of all my flyers. And I now have to go back home to work on my sermon. Who knows? You might be in it,' he said.

'Huh?'

'The parable of the *Big Issue* seller and the ginger cat, you must have heard of it?'

'Now you're taking the mickey, mate,' I said, giving him an affectionate slap on the back.

'Sorry. That's a habit of mine.'

We shook hands.

'A Merry Christmas to you, erm sorry, I don't know your name.'

'James.'

A Merry Christmas to you, James – and to you, Bob,' he said, gently stroking him on the back of the neck.

He was soon disappearing into the Tube station. It wasn't long before we followed in his footsteps.

For a change, Bob and I got the Tube back home.

It meant a longer walk at the end of our journey, but it also meant Bob could do his business in a small park that he liked. I could also walk off the pain in my leg which had returned after standing in the cold for so long.

Standing in the busy train carriage, I found myself staring at one of those 'Poems on the Underground'. I often read them. I found them quite inspiring. This one was a modern piece, however. I didn't quite get it. Instead I found myself thinking about my day and in particular my encounter with the guy from the church this evening.

Of course I'd heard the main message of that passage he'd recited before. I'd actually seen it in one of the Christmas cards that I'd been given. I'd thought it was just one of those seasonal slogans that someone, probably a Victorian, had come up with. I hadn't realised it came from the Bible. Which was pretty stupid of me, really.

I wasn't going to suddenly become a born-again Christian. He would have to deliver his Christmas Eve sermon without me in his congregation. But there was something admirable about the guy's quiet wisdom and his gentle, non-confrontational manner. It made such a pleasant change. He was also dead right about me; I had learned a precious lesson in these past couple of days. Giving out those cards had given me such a kick. It had been a real joy to see so many people's faces lighting up. He, or more accurately, the book of Acts, was spot on; sometimes it really was better to give than receive.

Chapter 6

The Office Party

There were now only two days until Christmas Day. I'd decided to spend a few hours busking in Covent Garden. I also had a few more Christmas cards to give out and was hoping that I might see one or two of my regulars from there.

It had been another long, slow bus journey because of the weather and, to make matters worse, Bob and I had been forced to get off in the middle of Oxford Street because of a diversion on the roads. It was like stepping into a scene from Bedlam.

With Christmas almost upon us, Oxford Street was crammed full of anxious-looking people, rushing frantically along as they tried to get their shopping finished.

Almost as soon as Bob had climbed on to my shoulders and we started walking, we passed a Salvation Army band and choir singing carols. One of the singers was carrying a placard that read 'Peace on Earth and Goodwill to All Men'. There wasn't much evidence of that in the air. As far as I could tell, it was a dog-eat-dog scramble to buy as much stuff as they possibly could and people didn't care who stood in their way. It wasn't a pretty sight.

People were overloaded with bags of all shapes and sizes. I saw one guy laden with what looked like a dozen giant sacks from fancy shops like Selfridges and John Lewis. Goodness only knows what he'd spent so far, but to judge by the harassed expression on his face as he shouted into his mobile phone, it wasn't enough.

'It's sold out everywhere I'm telling you,' he said, presumably to his equally wound-up wife. 'No, I tried that. I'm not joking. It's not anywhere.'

He looked like he was ready to have a heart attack. For a moment, I actually felt sorry for him and everyone else being driven to distraction by the last-minute rush. At least the desperation I had felt these past few days was mainly based on a real, physical need – to eat and keep warm. These people were in a frenzy over things that, in all likelihood, they or the recipients didn't really need at all. I didn't envy them. Quite the opposite in fact, I thought it was rather sad.

Bob was soon getting anxious at the number of people brushing past and bumping into us. He let out a loud *eeeew* when one fraught-looking lady knocked into my left shoulder spinning me through thirty degrees and almost dislodging him. She didn't stop to apologise, she just ploughed on down the road, weighed down with her precious Christmas cargo.

'Oh, sorry for being in your way,' I said sarcastically, watching her disappear and shaking my head at her rudeness.

'Come on, Bob, let's get out of this madness,' I said, turning off Oxford Street towards Soho Square. This was a shortcut we often took, partly because Bob enjoyed doing his business in the park. In the summer he also adored staring at the birds in the trees, but there was none of that today. The trees were barren and there was hardly a hint of green beneath the snow. Bob was picky about where he went to the toilet and took an age to find a patch of soil that wasn't as hard as iron.

We headed down towards Old Compton Street from where I intended to move on towards Cambridge Circus. It was much quieter here, thank goodness. This wasn't a shopping district; it was mostly bars and restaurants, many of which seemed to be winding down for Christmas. There were a few pockets of partygoers but it was pretty quiet, which was why the gravelly sound of a man's voice cut through the chilly afternoon air so easily.

'Oi, mate,' I heard it shout from an alleyway. I looked round and saw a figure emerging, flicking a cigarette to the floor as he walked.

He was a thickset, thirty-something guy dressed in a long, black leather coat with a thick tartan scarf around his neck. I knew pretty much instantly what he was up to; he was selling drugs.

'Ain't seen you in ages,' he said.

'Eh?'

'I remember you, man. I been away.'

I put two and two together. He must have been a dealer from years back when I was at my lowest. I couldn't remember him, which was hardly surprising. I'd been so far gone at that stage, I barely remembered what day of the week it was let alone who supplied me with my drugs. He'd probably been serving time in prison and had just re-emerged. Clearly he'd not mended his ways.

'Listen, wanna early Christmas present?'

He looked around, checking that the coast was clear, then produced a little white wrap which he proceeded to dangle in the air at arm's length in front of me.

'It's the business, man. It'll blow your head off.'

I immediately took a step back.

'*Whoah*, no thanks, mate. I'm clean these days.'

He looked at me for a second, a contrived, confused look on his face.

'It's on me. Free sample. Serious.'

'No, no.'

He looked cheesed off.

'Yeah? You sure?' he said, squinting at me, as if waiting for me to crack. But I wasn't going to give in, I'd come too far in my life to do that.

'Yeah, I'm totally sure,' I said, repositioning myself so that Bob and I could get past him.

That should have been the end of the conversation, but he obviously wasn't going to take no for an answer and placed himself in my way, blocking my exit. There was no one else around, which was a concern. I didn't know what he was capable of.

I knew the score here. Dealers like this prospered at Christmas time. An addict reaches this time of the year knowing there will be a 'drought' during the holidays and saves up extra money to buy enough supplies. The nature of addiction, however, means that the temptation to 'do' it all in a few days is always there. Dealers know this and capitalise on it – big time. They make fortunes on the back of addicts' dependency and weakness often by charging the same for smaller amounts as they would for larger ones at other times of the year.

This guy was on a fishing expedition. He wanted me to take the bait and then, once I'd bitten, he'd reel me in so that I would buy a load of his merchandise. A few years ago, I'd have been a prime 'mark'. There was no way I would have been able to resist a 'free' hit. I'd have been reeled in with ease. But I was a different person now. I wasn't going to fall for it. No matter what ideas this guy had.

'Look, mate. I'm good. I don't want anything. I just want to get on my way and get to work.'

It was inevitable, I guess, but his mood suddenly turned dark.

'Come on, man, come on. Let's do some business here. Let's help each other out,' he said, jutting out his chin and angling his head towards me.

He then pushed himself even closer, grabbing my arm with one hand then waving the little wrap closer with the other. He was now within inches of me – and Bob. That was his big mistake.

It happened in a split second, so fast, in fact, that I didn't see it properly. All I heard was an almighty *weeeeow* followed by a torrent of expletives. I then saw the guy dancing around, waving his hand violently.

It took me a few moments to work it out, but it was soon pretty clear what had happened.

I'd been aware of Bob throughout, he'd seemed restless from the moment the guy appeared.

As the guy had pushed himself forward, however, he'd clearly made a decision. Bob had taken a swipe at him and had caught him on the hand.

For a moment the guy just stood fixed to the spot, inspecting his hand – and us. He was in a state of shock, but then the shock gave way to anger.

'What's that f***ing thing, a f***ing tiger?' he said, leaning in towards us from a few feet away.

Bob hissed at him, forcing him back half a step.

'He's just watching out for me,' I said.

There was no blood, or at least I couldn't see any. He was lucky. Bob had kept his claws in. He had just given him a warning. If he wanted to he could have hurt him.

He started pacing around, swearing and waving his hand. He was clearly calculating his next move, but I'd already worked out mine.

I pushed past him and set off as quickly as I could down the road in the direction of Cambridge Circus. I didn't know whether he'd set off in pursuit, but I didn't want to risk it so I headed off down the icy pavement.. There was a group of people on the corner of the street about twenty to thirty yards away. I figured if I could get near to them the guy would definitely give up the ghost.

I felt Bob readjusting himself on my shoulder so that his tail was hanging over my front. He was looking back, obviously monitoring the guy's movement. We'd travelled about ten yards when he made a loud hissing noise that suggested the guy was following us, or at least thinking of doing so. I sped up, drawn by the prospect of the crowd that I could see in the street ahead.

It was one of those situations where time seemed to slow down. It could only have been seconds, but it felt like minutes before we got to the junction and the safety of the crowds gathered there.

I breathed a huge sigh of relief. We were in the clear.

It took me a few minutes to calm down. My heart was pounding. It was the sort of situation I'd found myself in almost on a daily basis when I was an addict. But those days were long gone and I had been thrown by the guy's aggression. Dealers like that really were the scum of the earth, as far as I was concerned. They preyed on the weakest and most vulnerable. They thought nothing of taking every penny that a homeless person had to his or her name. When they locked him up they should have thrown away the key.

My emotions were in a jumble for the rest of our journey to Neal Street. I was shaken, but I was also relieved. Most of all, though, I was grateful. Grateful to Bob.

This wasn't the first time he'd taken a dislike to

someone who he sensed was up to no good. At Angel and around Covent Garden, he'd always had a knack for picking out people who he instinctively knew were a threat. It was a kind of radar. It had clearly been operating here, thank goodness.

I was determined that the incident wasn't going to ruin my day, however. I was feeling so much more positive about the world. I didn't want to lose that feeling. So I found myself a spot on James Street and started busking Christmas songs.

My usual playlist was full of modern, slightly dark songs. I sang stuff by Johnny Cash and Nine Inch Nails. 'Wonderwall' by Oasis was always a favourite. But I knew the usual set-list wasn't really appropriate at Christmas so I'd been practising a few, more seasonal songs on the guitar at home. I figured that people wanted to hear something cheery at this time of the year, especially as it was so cold. I wanted to play stuff that maybe warmed them up and put a Christmassy smile on their faces. I also wanted them to stop and donate some money, of course. Again, it was a reflection of how I'd started to embrace the spirit of Christmas a little more. I'd never have dreamt of playing that sort of music a few years ago. It would have been anathema to me.

I began with the most obvious song, 'Jingle Bells'. It was really easy to play and had a jaunty rhythm to it when played on the guitar. Also, everybody knew it. I also played 'I Saw Mommy Kissing Santa Claus' and a speeded-up, almost punky version of 'White Christmas', which people seemed to like.

Standing there singing for hours on end can get very boring so I also began to improvise.

Bob was there in his cute Santa Paws outfit so when I was singing 'Jingle Bells', for instance, I made up lines like 'The bell on Bob's hat rings' and 'Over the fields Bob goes' and 'Bobbing all the way, on a one-horse open sleigh.'

I didn't know if people even got it. How were they to know his name was Bob? But I didn't worry about it too much. I wanted to have fun and entertain people in the process. It was Christmas and I was really getting in the spirit by now.

Not everyone shared that spirit, of course. There were a few drunks around, inevitably.

Every now and again a gang of blokes or an office party would tumble out of the big pubs on James Street in high spirits.

Some appreciated my music. After I'd been there for an hour or so, a group of men and women in office clothes came out after what must have been a very long lunch and started jigging away to 'Jingle Bells'. When it got to the chorus, they all linked arms as if doing the hokey cokey and started singing along.

Not one of them dropped a penny into my guitar case, but that was to be expected really. They were having a party. Why spoil it with depressing thoughts about other people?

Unfortunately, there were one or two people who felt the need to have a go at me. It was the usual stuff, the same sorts of insults I'd been hearing for years: 'Get a proper job you lazy so-and-so'; 'Your cat could sing better than you'; 'Get a haircut, you bloody hippy'. It wasn't very creative. After all these years I wish I could say it washed over me like water off a duck's back, but I couldn't. It always hurt. People had absolutely no idea what my life was like or how I had come to be here. Even worse they weren't interested in knowing.

Fortunately there were enough decent souls around to compensate. After a couple of hours I'd accumulated about £20. I'd already had to run the gauntlet of a few of the local 'Covent Guardians' who policed the Piazza and the surrounding area to make sure the people performing there had the correct licences. One had moved me on but I'd gone around the corner and waited for a little while before returning. I knew my luck wouldn't hold for much longer, however, so I decided to cut my losses and head off.

On the way back down Neal Street I remembered that I had a couple of Christmas cards still in my rucksack.

I hadn't forgotten the pledge I'd made a couple of days ago. We walked past a lovely old Italian cafe and sandwich shop near where I used to busk before I started concentrating on selling *The Big Issue*. It was run by a nice family, one of whom, a middle-aged lady, used to slip me the odd free cheese roll. I stuck my head in to see if she was still there. To my delight she was.

She didn't know what to say when I produced a card and handed it over.

'Sorry about this, it's about two years too late, but Merry Christmas,' I said. 'And thanks for being so kind to me.'

Her face broke into a broad smile when she opened the card.

'Yes, I remember you,' she said. 'Haven't seen you two for a while. How are you doing?'

'All right,' I said, gesturing at Bob. 'Thanks to this little fellow.'

I decided to head back to Angel. I wanted to buy Belle a Christmas present and was keen to check out the shops there. I preferred them to those in Covent Garden. They were quieter – and a lot cheaper too.

The light was already fading fast, dragging the

temperature down with it. It felt like there was yet more snow in the air. On the Tube journey back Bob had begun making the telltale gestures that told me he wanted to go to the toilet again. So when we got to Angel I walked over to the small park at Islington Green.

The place was deserted, which was hardly surprising given that even the park benches were still layered with snow. As I stood there smoking a quick cigarette, the sound of the wind whistling eerily through the barren branches of the trees was so strong it even drowned out the drone of the ever-present traffic. I could have been standing in the middle of the countryside, not the heart of London.

Bob usually relished the chance to root around in the bushes here, sniffing for mice or birds but, just as in Soho, he wasn't interested in hanging around today. Within a couple of minutes of disappearing into the overgrowth, he had reappeared ready to jump back on my shoulder.

I crossed the road and took a turn down Camden Passage, the narrow lane that leads back to the Tube station. It would be a little more sheltered there, I figured. The alleyway was surprisingly busy, presumably with last-minute shoppers and partygoers visiting its trendy cafes, restaurants, art and antique shops. I wouldn't ordinarily bother looking in any of them, but about halfway along the passage there was a little side alley where there were a few flea-market-like stores. It was a long shot, but I wanted to see if there was anything I could get for Belle.

The prices on most of the objects were ridiculous. I could never have afforded any of them. But then I saw a shop with large trays displaying jewellery. To my surprise, the prices weren't too scary. A lot of the items were £10 or under.

'Shall we take a look, Bob?' I said.

The shopkeeper was very friendly and didn't object to Bob being in his store, in fact he seemed pleased to see him.

'Good afternoon, sir. What a handsome fellow you have there.'

I couldn't remember the last time someone had called me sir. Or the last time a shopkeeper had been quite so welcoming. I usually felt their eyes burning into me. I could almost see the thoughts forming in their mind. 'Who is this scruffy character? What's he up to, he must be planning to steal something?'

Encouraged by this I spent a few minutes rummaging through the tray of rings, necklaces and earrings.

One item jumped out at me. They were metallic, sculpture-like earrings. I reckoned I knew Belle's taste pretty well so I was sure she'd like them.

There wasn't a price tag on them, which worried me. My feeling was always that if I had to ask for a price it meant that I couldn't afford it. But I decided to risk it.

'How much for these?' I said, pointing.

I was pleasantly surprised by the answer.

'Oh, they're eighteen pounds.'

It was still a lot of money, for me at least, and it must have shown.

'But go on, I'll let you have them for less. What shall we say? Fifteen?'

'Done,' I said with a smile that must have told him he'd made my day.

The shopkeeper even put them in a nice little box and a smart, stiff white paper gift bag.

'Merry Christmas to you both,' he said as we left.

'And the same to you.'

I felt quite pleased with myself. Belle was such a good friend to me yet I hadn't ever bought her a proper present. In fact, I hadn't really bought anyone a meaningful present before, so strange had my Christmases been. It was a sign of how my attitude was slowly changing. My inner Scrooge was definitely on the wane, I laughed to myself as I left the shop clutching my purchase.

'Better earn some money to pay for this,' I said to Bob, half joking.

My supply of *Big Issue* magazines was almost all gone so, with Bob on my shoulder, I crossed Islington High Street and headed for the spot on the pavement where the co-ordinators were usually based.

There was no sign of the trolley where they stored the magazines. Instead around ten vendors in red bibs were standing there, stamping their feet, drawing on cigarettes and sipping from cans of beer and cola.

'So what's the story?' I asked one of them, gesturing at the spot where the trolley normally stood.

'Christmas Eve tomorrow, so they've finished today. Lucky sods,' he said.

'So where do we get papers from if we need them?' I said.

'Covent Garden,' another of the vendors said.

'That's annoying, I've just come from there,' I said.

'Or go all the way to Head Office in bloody Vauxhall,' added a third vendor.

This wasn't great news, particularly for those who only worked in this part of London. I tended to visit Covent Garden in any case and I knew the co-ordinator there so was not overly worried. That might not be so easy for the others. I felt sorry for them.

One of them looked pretty crestfallen. I could

tell that he was relying on it to get through the next few days. I knew what a tightrope act it was. I hoped he wouldn't fall.

Another vendor, Vince, a guy I knew in passing, appeared. I had seen him working occasionally at the far end of Upper Street, not far from Highbury Corner. He had always struck me as a larger-than-life character.

'What's this, the office Christmas party?'

One or two of the vendors laughed, others just looked at him blankly. They clearly didn't get the joke.

'Well if no one's got any papers to sell, why don't we go for a drink? 'Tis the season to be jolly and all that,' Vince said.

A few of the guys shook their heads. I suspected one or two of them might have been recovering alcoholics and didn't want to get involved for obvious reasons. Others probably didn't have too much money. I knew the feeling. I could under-stand why they weren't exactly in the mood to be 'jolly'.

I thought it was a good idea, however. We were no different to all the other groups of co-workers getting together in London as we spoke. Covent Garden had been full of them, as I'd seen. Whether they were bankers in the City or street cleaners in Camden, they were marking the end of the working year and the beginning of the Christmas holiday together. Why shouldn't we?

I could only see one problem.

'They won't let a bunch of scruffy *Big Issue* sellers into a pub. Especially as I've got this fellow with me,' I said.

'No, you're right. But I've got an idea,' Vince said with a wink.

A few vendors melted away, but the rest of us crossed Upper Street and followed Vince to a small, private park off Camden Passage. Its gates were always open; I'd popped in there with Bob a couple of times. There was a pub nearby.

We organised a whip round, with everyone putting a fiver in.

'So who's the most likely to get served?' Vince said.

We nominated a guy called Gavin. I had no idea about his background, but he had a posh voice and a decent haircut. He took off his tabard and headed into the pub with another vendor in tow.

They soon appeared with a tray full of pints of beer.

'Here you go, guys,' Gavin announced.

'Cheers,' Vince said. 'Happy Christmas to us all.'

It was cold and there was a lot of foot-stamping to keep warm. I let Bob wander off to explore the overgrowth. The snow had been cleared away so there was more to explore than across the road in the park on Islington Green.

Conversation was slow to begin with, mainly about our day-to-day experiences selling the magazine.

A couple of guys were complaining about the quality of the content, something I'd noticed myself.

'There's a lot of rubbish in there at the moment. It's no wonder people aren't buying it so much,' one said. There were lots of nods to that.

There were a few awkward silences as we all stood around sipping at our, by now, ice-cold beers. They were, I knew, a little bit wary of me because Bob and I had begun to get a little bit of attention. There were a couple of videos about us on the internet and they'd all seen an article about us in the local newspaper, the *Islington Tribune*. I'd had a few dirty looks and heard some jealous mutterings from other vendors afterwards. A couple of vendors had also seen me when I'd had my first meeting with the writer who was going to help me with the book. We'd sat outside shivering as I explained the story of how Bob and I had met. The sight of me sitting with a guy with a notebook had drawn a few glances. I knew that it was all pie in the sky really. The odds on me becoming an author were on a par with those on Bob becoming Mayor of London. In other words, zero. But they weren't to know that. As far as they were concerned, I was some kind of 'celebrity'.

Inevitably, it came up at one point.

'It's all right for you two,' one guy said when we were talking about how hard it had been to sell magazines during the past week or two of Arctic weather. 'You are famous now.'

I recognised him. He was an elderly guy, whom I'd seen selling the magazine on Camden Passage a couple of times.

'Doesn't pay the gas bill though,' I smiled. 'Trust me, I'm in the same boat as the rest of you.'

'I doubt that,' he said. We chatted for a while. He didn't go into the details of his life story; few *Big Issue* vendors ever do. Our stories were often variations on the same themes: addiction, broken homes, bad childhoods, the usual sad stuff. He told me that he was living in a shelter at the moment. The only problem was that it had a limit on the number of nights he could stay there and he was fast approaching that number.

'So where are you going to spend Christmas then?' I asked him.

He just shrugged his shoulders.

'Your guess is as good as mine.'

I knew how that felt. I'd been in that position myself years earlier when I'd been a 'rough sleeper' moving from one night shelter to another or sleeping on pavements around central London. It made me realise how fortunate I was to have my little flat. It wasn't much but it was certainly more than this guy had. For a moment I thought about offering him a space on my floor, but I soon realised that was a non-starter. Belle was coming over for part of the Christmas holiday. There was no room at the inn. Our conversation was interrupted by another voice.

'Anyone got a spare cigarette?' asked the youngest of the vendors, a blond guy I'd seen around a few times. He couldn't have been more than twenty-five or twenty-six.

I'd been a bit wary of him when I'd seen him. He looked like he was too young and not streetwise enough to sell the magazine. But he seemed pleasant enough today. As it happened I had a couple of cigarettes left in my packet.

'Here you go,' I said.

'Cheers, James,' he said.

I was surprised. I didn't even think he knew my name. We got chatting and he asked me about Bob and how we'd got together. I'd told the story a million times already, but was happy to do so again.

'I had a ginger cat when I was a kid. Called him Fozzie, after Fozzie Bear in the Muppets,' he said.

Bob was normally wary of other vendors but he let the guy stroke him.

'He's cool.'

'Anyone for another?' Vince said after a while.

'One more, then I've got to head home,' I said.

Gavin went back into the pub and repeated the same trick again.

As everyone loosened up a bit we started to enjoy ourselves. Vince turned out to be something of a comedian and did great impressions of some of the *Big Issue*'s outreach workers. There was a lot of laughter. I felt pleased. I'd had more than my fair share of trouble with other vendors; I'd been given suspensions for 'floating', or selling the magazine away from official pitches, after being reported by a couple of them and I'd also had people try to muscle their way on to my pitches both at Covent Garden and here at Angel in the past. Pitches at Tube stations had traditionally been regarded as a waste of time because people are always in such a hurry there but, with Bob's help, I'd made them both a success. A couple of vendors had fancied their chances of cashing in on that success, mistakenly, as it turned out.

So I had given most of them a wide berth during the past year. I felt uneasy in their company; I guess I didn't trust them. A couple of hours in their company today had made me re-evaluate them. They were no different to me, really. They were no better or worse as human beings. Deep down they were just as proud, paranoid and vulnerable as me, I felt sure. They just wanted to survive. They just wanted to get through Christmas with a roof over their head and some food in their stomachs. It was an object lesson really. You shouldn't judge a book by its cover.

I was the first to leave. Vince tried to persuade me to stay but I wanted to get home with Bob before the weather turned again, as it was predicted to do. It was also really cold and I could tell Bob was ready to head home to the warmth of the flat. We hopped on the bus. I put my guitar up on the rack and my rucksack beside me. I then put the bag with Belle's present under my feet, so that it would be safe.

It had been another long and eventful day. I felt exhausted and, with the additional help of the two pints and the warmth of the bus's heater which was blowing on my legs, I'd had no problem in nodding off to sleep. I only woke up as we were approaching our bus stop back in Tottenham. It may well have been Bob who gave me a nudge. He had an in-built mechanism for knowing when we were almost home and had done so on more than one occasion before when I'd dropped off at the end of a hard day.

Realising where I was, I reacted on autopilot. I hit the red 'stop' button, quickly grabbed my guitar and rucksack, scooped Bob up on to my shoulders and ran off the bus. It was dark and the icy pavements were still tricky to negotiate. It was only when I was approaching home that it hit me.

'Oh no,' I said. 'Belle's present.'

I was furious with myself. I also felt like a complete idiot. How could I have been so stupid? Why hadn't I spotted that I didn't have the bag on me? After all the good things that had happened in the last forty-eight hours, it took the wind out of my

sails a little. It wasn't the first time I'd lost a bag on the bus or Tube. I had a habit of misplacing things. But that didn't make it any easier. This was different, this was something special. Back home that night, I slept fitfully.

Chapter 7

The Ghost of Christmas Past

'Stay there for a while, Bob,' I said, draining the last of my tea and throwing on my coat.

He wasn't keen on being left alone, I could tell.

'Don't worry, I won't be long,' I said, giving him a reassuring ruffle of the thicket of fur on the back of his neck before heading out the door.

It was Christmas Eve but I had got up early. I couldn't have slept in late, in any case. My mind was still endlessly replaying the moment I'd got out of my seat on the bus. I still couldn't believe I'd been so careless.

There had been another light snow overnight. Outside I could see that the cars parked on the road had a fresh dusting of what looked like icing sugar on their roofs. We were definitely going to have a white Christmas.

The weather wasn't going to deter me, however. The local bus garage was about half a mile away. I'd been prepared to walk but luckily a bus came by almost immediately and I was there within minutes.

The fleet of red buses in the garage were already streaked with a new coat of white. Drivers were busily de-icing their windscreens while others were scraping the snow away from the parking areas with shovels.

'Where's the Lost and Found Office, mate?' I asked one of them. He pointed in the direction of a hangar-like building. Inside there was a small booth where I could see there was a lady on the telephone. She spotted me and held up her hand as if to say 'wait a moment'.

When she eventually deigned to speak to me she couldn't have been less helpful.

'Did anyone hand in a white gift bag last night?' I said. 'About this size,' I added, holding my hands about a foot apart.

'I don't know,' she said.

'Well, who does know?,' I said, slightly irritated.

'Try Baker Street,' she said, in a monosyllabic grunt.

'Baker Street?'

'Yes. Anything we find here gets sent to the main Transport for London Lost Property Office for all the Underground and buses. It's next to Baker Street Tube station.'

'Oh, OK. Is it open today?'

'Don't know,' she said. 'But even if someone found it here last night, it might not be there yet. To be honest, I'd give it a day or so.'

'But it's Christmas Eve. It's a Christmas present.'

She just shrugged her shoulders. She clearly couldn't care less.

'Well do you at least know what time the office closes?' I said.

'Half four normally,' she said.

My heart sank. I hadn't planned on going into the centre of London again. I was tired of the crowds and the constant rush. I was fed up with some people's selfishness and, yes, sheer greed at this time of the year. I was ready to take it easy and to start my Christmas, but it seemed like I had little choice in the matter.

I thought I'd give it a few hours in the hope that the bag would make its way to Baker Street. In the meantime I decided to head into Covent Garden. I popped back to the flat and collected my guitar and the couple of spare *Big Issue* magazines I'd left there. Bob had clearly missed me when I had gone out earlier and was keen to come so I slipped him into his Santa Paws outfit again.

'What do you think, mate? Might as well give it one more outing before we put it in mothballs ready for next year.'

I couldn't face another epic bus trip so we walked to the Tube station. The trains were running well and we were in Covent Garden within the hour.

The Piazza was packed with people soaking up the Christmas atmosphere. The mood was vibrant and very jolly. I found a good spot at the top of James Street and started playing the jaunty 'Jingle Bells' stuff again. Small knots of people stopped to say hello and sometimes sing along.

One family stayed with us for about ten minutes, the children singing along with me. We all enjoyed ourselves.

Bob was on top form and was again inviting me to do tricks with him. There were lots of *oooohs* and *aaaahs* as he stood on his hind legs to snatch a treat from my fingertips. He must have been photo-graphed a hundred times in the space of a couple of hours. Goodness knows where those photos would soon be spread on the internet. There were already dozens of photos and videos on sites like YouTube. 'At this rate, he is going to get into the *Guinness*

Book of Records as the world's most photographed cat, I laughed to myself, not really believing it, of course.

Two of our regulars passed by on their way home after a half day in the office. I had a couple of cards left still and gave them one each.

'All ready for the big day?' one of them, a middle-aged lady called Patricia asked.

'As ready as we will ever be,' I said. 'How about you?'

Her face sank.

'Going home now to start on a meal for fourteen people tomorrow afternoon. Absolutely dreading it.'

'Oh dear. I'm glad it's just me and Bob for dinner at our place. Much more straightforward,' I smiled.

'Sounds lovely, can I join you?' she laughed. I got the impression that she was only half-joking.

By 2 p.m. or so the crowds were thinning as everyone began heading home to begin their Christmas, so I decided to follow suit.

'Come on, Bob, it's Christmas, mate, time to call it a day,' I said.

For a while we just walked around, taking in the atmosphere, like a normal pair of Londoners. Covent Garden looked – and smelled – absolutely beautiful. The Christmas lights were a riot of colour and the air was thick with the smell of roast chestnuts and mulled wine. There were still a few street entertainers at work around the marketplace in the middle of the Piazza. With Bob on his lead, I took a stroll. Some of the stall-holders were packing up for Christmas while others were offering last-minute discounts in order to clear their stock. I took a look at a couple of jewellery stalls on the off-chance that they had something that might replace the earrings I'd left on the bus, but there was nothing that caught my eye. I was also reluctant to fork out another £15.

There were all sorts of tempting things in the shops but I decided I wasn't going to spend any money. I had the Marks and Spencer voucher I'd been given so headed there instead. As a treat, I bought myself a jar of onion chutney. I was tempted to buy a smart Christmas pudding but decided against it. Belle was coming over on Boxing Day for our traditional feast and I knew she was bringing one with her. I resisted the temptation. Just. Instead I bought a nice box of chocolates, just so that I had something nice and Christmassy to give her on Boxing Day if the present didn't show up at Baker Street. I also had an idea for another, home-made present which I'd work on later this evening. By now I'd begun to put the loss of Belle's present in better perspective. It wasn't the end of the world, I told myself. I had suffered much bigger blows in recent years. Belle, of all people, would understand.

The sound of another Salvation Army band playing carols was drifting across the Piazza. They were singing 'Silent Night'.

'All is calm, all is bright.'

It was true, I told myself. All was calm. The future was bright, well, certainly compared to my all-too-recent past. I had a lot to be grateful for.

I'd let Bob walk on his lead so that he could explore the nooks and crannies under the market stalls. When I heard the clock strike 2.30 p.m., however, I scooped him up and headed out of the market past a guy on a unicycle who was entertaining the crowds at the west end of the Piazza.

'Come on, Bob. Let's just see if that bag has shown up, then we will head home,' I said.

I was going to head towards Leicester Square but suddenly Bob started making telltale noises that he wanted to go to the toilet. I knew a couple of spots that he could use, so headed in a different direction.

I decided to cut through Neal's Yard and emerged on to Monmouth Street, opposite the Covent Garden Hotel. The sight of a figure lying on the pavement across the road stopped me in my tracks.

It was, I could tell from a distance, a young man. He was lying on a cardboard box and wrapped in a threadbare blue sleeping bag and a grey blanket. His body was curled up against the biting cold. I crossed the road to take a closer look. He was a young guy, no more than nineteen or twenty years of age. He had a woollen hat on and was wearing a pair of ripped mittens. His face was covered in grime and was red raw from the cold while his hair and beard were wild and unruly. He probably had lice which was a common affliction among rough sleepers given the lack of washing facilities on the streets. He looked like he hadn't had a shower in a month.

I was shocked, not by the fact he was sleeping on the streets, but by the fact that he was living rough here, at this exact spot. It was eerie. It had been here, at this precise place at this precise time, that I had experienced the worst Christmas of my life.

At that point I had been at my absolute lowest ebb. I had been eking out an existence on the streets for about a year. I'd tried to get a job to break the downward spiral but no one was willing to give me a break. I'd turned to petty crime to survive, shoplifting meat from supermarkets and reselling it in pubs to make enough money to feed my drug addiction. That was the be-all-and-end-all of my existence at that point. Heroin completely controlled me. It was my only friend and comfort, the only source I had for numbing all my emotions. It was all I could think about. I was in a really bad way.

And so it was that on Christmas Eve that year, as everybody else had headed home to be with their families, I had come to Monmouth Street and laid down my piece of cardboard for the night at this same spot. There was a reason why it was popular with rough sleepers. The patch of pavement was next door to the swanky Covent Garden Hotel, right in front of a wall where there were two large vents. I could see that they were still there now. The vents extracted or pumped out air from the kitchens of the hotel. The air, while not exactly hot, was certainly several degrees warmer than the outside temperature. It made a huge difference if you were trying to get a decent night's sleep, especially during the winter.

I had slept here a few times, much to the annoyance of some of the local shopkeepers. One of them really disliked me. She was the kind of person that had absolutely no sympathy for anyone who was sleeping rough or selling *The Big Issue*. As far as she was concerned we were all losers who had somehow ended up in the same boat by choice. She had no interest in how we might have arrived at this point in our lives or whether we needed help. We were just blemishes on the landscape. I'm sure if she could have had her way we'd have been cleared up by the garbage collectors.

On more than one occasion she'd sworn at me

when she'd seen me near her shop in the morning. When I'd protested, she'd let out a stream of expletives.

Fortunately, that Christmas Eve, however, there was no sign of her or anyone else. Every shop on the street had closed by the time I arrived there, early in the evening. While the rest of the world went to their Christmas Eve carol services, gathered around the television and ate big family meals, I wrapped myself up in my sleeping bag and lay there, shivering and feeling desperately lonely. Not a single soul stopped to ask if I was all right or needed any help. It was a long and desperate night.

I eventually fell asleep and woke up around mid-morning on Christmas Day. The place was bizarrely quiet, as if London had been evacuated. A few people were coming in and out of the hotel next door, but otherwise it was a ghost town.

I hadn't really planned anything, I rarely did then. But I knew there were a couple of charity shelters that might be serving Christmas lunch. I figured I'd try to get into one of them.

I gathered up my cardboard and belongings and got ready to move off. As I shuffled past the Covent Garden Hotel, I saw a group of people in the window. They were dressed up to the nines and had flutes of champagne in their hands. My guess was that they were there for lunch and were just having the first drink of the day. I didn't begrudge them their meal. I knew that they worked hard through the rest of the year. They had earned it. I didn't want to spoil it for them.

I was about to walk on when one of them spotted me. He just looked blankly out, as if I wasn't there. It just underlined that feeling that I was invisible, a non-person. I didn't even merit a raised glass or a Merry Christmas.

I felt pretty sorry for myself, but if I'd imagined I couldn't get much lower, I was wrong. Relations with my father were at an all-time low at that point. I'd effectively gone missing for the best part of a year and he'd been understandably furious with me when I'd resurfaced just a few weeks earlier. I'd telephoned him at his home in south London. At first he'd refused to come to the phone, and when he did he unleashed a string of expletives at me. He'd had every right to do so, of course. He had been worried sick about me. We'd exchanged some heated words again the previous week when we'd spoken and it had been clear that I wasn't wanted at his house this Christmas. He was also going through problems in his marriage to his then wife Sue, whom he would soon divorce.

I passed a phone box and decided to give him a call, reversing the charges. I perhaps shouldn't have been surprised by the reception I got. Sue answered the phone.

'Oh, Merry Christmas, James,' she said.

'Merry Christmas to you too. Is my dad there?' I said.

I could hear her muffling the receiver and then heard a brief exchange of words. I then heard Sue back on the phone, nervously clearing her throat.

'I'm really sorry, James, but he doesn't want to talk to you,' she said.

'OK.'

I felt close to tears. I knew I'd been a terrible disappointment – and more to the point, a huge worry – during the course of the preceding year. But I couldn't hide my hurt.

'You all right, James?' Sue said.

'Yeah, I'm fine,' I said, pulling myself together. 'Happy Christmas.'

I then hung up.

I wandered in the direction of Dean Street, in Soho, where I knew there was a temporary refuge run by the charity Centrepoint. They knew me because I'd slept there several times.

There were a couple of guys standing at the door, one of whom recognised me.

'Oh hello, James, Merry Christmas, mate.'

'And to you,' I'd said. 'Any chance of Christmas lunch?'

'We're pretty full actually,' the other guy said but his colleague interrupted, nodding as if to say, *It's OK, I know him.*

'Yeah, of course, James. Come on in.'

London was dotted with refuges like this at Christmas time. They provided a basic living space for homeless people and served Christmas dinner for those who wanted it. It was a far cry from the fare on offer at the Covent Garden Hotel, but at that point I didn't much care. There was some ham and a turkey crown, roast potatoes, sprouts, some stuffing and gravy. It hardly compared to the feasts being eaten around London and the rest of the country, but I wolfed down a couple of plates in no time at all then followed it up with some Christmas pudding.

There were around three dozen people sitting around the makeshift table. I recognised one or two faces but most of them were strangers to me. I could tell a lot of them were addicts and users which put me on my guard immediately. I'd had some bad experiences staying in shelters where they were sleeping. They would steal the clothes you were wearing if they could. I hadn't sunk that low yet.

Along with a couple of dozen others, I sat around for the afternoon and played a few board games. Everything had been donated by the public so most of the games were incomplete. We used Coke bottle tops and buttons as pieces. There were trays of chocolates on the table. I helped myself to as many as I could eat.

Later on we watched a bit of television. I remember that *Who Wants to be a Christmas Millionaire* had just begun and was on at some point during the day. In the quiz, of course, contestants can take a 50/50 gamble. I couldn't appreciate it at the time, of course, but in a way that was precisely what I was doing with my life. In fact the odds weren't that good.

That night I went to bed in the men's dormitory and had another fix. In the run up to Christmas, I had somehow got hold of enough money to get myself a week's supply. I'd spent every penny I'd made on it; I'd not even bothered to eat properly. I had divided it up into a dozen little sachets that I planned to ration over the coming days. Addicts generally aren't any good at rationing stuff out like that, however. I did it all in the space of forty-eight hours or so. I spent Christmas night and Boxing Day in the shelter but barely registered either day. They were lost to me. Again, looking back on it, I can see that I was taking ridiculous risks. Christmas time was notorious for 'stingers', drugs that had been mixed with ground-down breeze blocks and goodness knows what else. I'd heard tales of junkies dying from taking stuff at this time of the year. I had bought my stuff from some very dodgy characters. My odds had probably been a lot less attractive than 50/50 but somehow I survived, but only to do the same thing all over again. That was the vicious circle I was trapped in.

By the time I was kicked out of the refuge on December 27th, I was keeping myself going with what addicts call 'filters'. I had saved up bits of cotton wool that had residues of heroin in them which I then washed to extract enough for a small fix. It was like using old tea bags. Just more desperate.

My priority had been to score some more. Again, I managed to raise the money I needed to keep feeding my habit. I always did then. You do when you are an addict. It feels like it's a matter of life or death, which, in a way, it is. I remember seeing myself reflected in the window of a big department store that week. I barely recognised the broken, bedraggled, sickly looking character that looked back at me.

As I looked at the figure lying here on Monmouth Street, a montage of images from that time passed through my mind. What had people seen when they'd walked down this same street a dozen years ago? Had anyone tried to help me? Probably not. Had anyone even noticed me? Probably not. The truth was, I would never know.

I couldn't get over the fact that this guy was lying in the exact same spot, on the same day of the year. He was even around my age at that time and looked a little like me. It was as if I'd been given a window back in time, as if I was actually looking at myself. I felt like I'd walked into Dickens' *Christmas Carol* and been shown the Ghost of Christmas Past. It really freaked me out.

Bob must have been shaken by it as well because he jumped down and started pacing around, as if worried about the guy's welfare. He was right to be concerned, of course. It was so cold, he could easily freeze to death if he stayed here for too long.

The Centrepoint that had taken me in no longer existed but I knew charities like Crisis at Christmas had taken over schools and empty buildings for the duration of the holidays. They were offering clean beds and decent meals for the coming few days. They probably had outreach workers on the streets looking for people in this guy's position as we spoke. He needed to find one of these people and get to one of their shelters.

I was pretty sure the guy wasn't on drugs; he just looked like he was exhausted and sleeping. I gave him a gentle nudge in the ribs. At first he didn't respond, which worried me, but fortunately after a while he responded, groaning.

'Uuuh. Whaaadya want?'

I looked in my pocket. I didn't have much, about £20 or so. I knew I had a little bit more cash saved up at home so I slipped £10 into his pocket.

'Hey, mate, there's a tenner, go and get a cup of coffee and get yourself to a shelter.'

He groaned again, but eventually acknowledged me.

'Yeah, man. OK.'

'Seriously, you won't make it through the night if you stay there. It's just too cold.'

'OK.'

'OK, look after yourself,' I said before heading off.

As Bob and I headed down the road, I kept turning around to check whether he had moved. I had a feeling he'd just tried to appease me. To my relief I saw him gathering together his stuff. As I approached Seven Dials, Bob and I watched him disappear in the other direction, a ghostly figure shuffling along in the snow.

Bob and I got the Tube to Baker Street. It was mercifully quiet on the train; the commuters and last-minute shoppers were thin on the ground. The countdown to Christmas was almost over.

The Lost Property Office was next door to the entrance to the Tube. I saw immediately that it was closed. There was a sign saying that they would be open again on the first working day after the holidays. That was going to be the following Tuesday. My hopes of retrieving the earrings were gone.

I wasn't the only disappointed customer. A young guy in a baseball jacket walked up to the glass door, giving it a tug as if he expected it to open. His head dropped as he read the notice.

'I don't believe this. Someone told me it was open until 4.30 p.m. today,' he said.

'Same here, mate,' I said.

He picked up his mobile looking like he was close to tears. He then trudged off, crestfallen. He just kept muttering,' I don't know . . . I don't know.'

I was disappointed. Part of me felt optimistic that the package would turn up at some point. It would only be a few months until Belle's birthday, I told myself. I can save it until then. I had a tenner in my pocket so I took a quick scout around the stores on Baker Street but there was precious little. Most of the shops belonged to chains and were selling bland, mass-manufactured stuff. That really wasn't Belle's cup of tea at all. Even worse, it would look like I'd just grabbed something at the last minute. That wasn't what I wanted.

The weather was looking ominous again, so rather than catch the bus I decided to jump back on the Tube and headed back up to Tottenham. Suddenly it was surprisingly busy with commuters as well as people who had probably been down on Oxford Street doing some last-minute shopping. The sight of the smart gift bags dotted around the carriage reminded me of my stupidity.

The atmosphere was very lively. People seemed to be having fun. A group of Australian lads got on at one point that were clearly in the party spirit and singing away. It wasn't a very Christmassy song. It was a funny version of that old song 'Ten Green Bottles . . .' – 'Ten Kangaroos Sitting on the Fence . . .'. At first the carriage was reluctant to join in but there was something so infectious and silly about the song and the young guys that others were soon singing along.

Even I couldn't resist and mumbled along to a couple of verses.

'And if one kangaroo, should accidentally fall . . . there'll be three kangaroos sitting on the fence.'

It took me back to my childhood in Western Australia where the sight of kangaroos was really common. I couldn't remember seeing one sitting on a fence though.

As we emerged back into the fading light, Bob started getting agitated.

'Not again, Bob, you've been once already,' I said. He was adamant, however. I knew that he'd only get more grouchy if I didn't let him do his business so I went on the lookout for a suitable spot.

The walk home took us past a large building site. The workers had knocked off for the day, probably for the Christmas holiday. Their dump trucks and concrete mixers stood silent. The site was deserted. I spotted a gap in the fencing and squeezed through with Bob. He had already spotted a large area of loosened soil so I let him get on with it.

I noticed a pile of broken masonry or concrete. It looked like a pavement or a wall had been demolished and left in a huge heap. For the first time in days, the sun had shown its face. In among the carnage, something caught my eye. I was sort of glinting in the dying light. I leaned down and picked it up.

It was a piece of concrete, roughly the size of the palm of my hand. It was smooth on one side but rough and broken on the other. What was really interesting about it was that the exposed bit was studded with multi-coloured stones, some of them crystal-like. The flat surface was coloured too; it looked like it had bits of graffiti on it. It could easily have been a piece of modern art in a gallery.

'Hmmm,' I said to myself. 'This is kind of cool.'

I was still holding the stone up to the light when Bob reappeared, ready to go. He looked at me standing there with a random piece of rock and gave me what looked like a quizzical stare. If I didn't know better, I'd have thought he was saying, 'What's that thing in your hand?'

I was about to drop the concrete back on to the pile of rubble when the thought came to me.

'Belle will love this,' I said to myself.

'Hold on a second, Bob,' I said, then I unzipped my rucksack and popped the concrete inside.

We were safely installed in the flat by 4 p.m. It felt good to shut the door on the world, for a few days at least. I had a long hot bath and made us some dinner. I cooked the gammon which I ate with some potatoes and carrots. It was lovely. I even gave Bob a couple of pieces of the gammon, which he snaffled down. We then settled down for the evening.

There was very little that I wanted to watch on the television. The schedule was full of movies I'd seen before or special editions of series that I didn't really like. But I had other plans anyway . . .

I spent half an hour working on a present idea that I had for Belle. I also had a little wrapping paper left so I used it to cover the piece of concrete, then tied a little bow around it. When I placed it with the other presents in the small stack under the tree, Bob immediately jumped up to explore. I couldn't help laughing as he repeatedly tried to nudge it but each time it stubbornly refused to move. He must have made a dozen attempts to shift it before he finally gave up.

I couldn't help smiling to myself. It was such a simple pleasure. I thought: Who needs Christmas Eve television when you can watch such an endless source of entertainment as Bob?

Chapter 8

A Gift from Bob

Waaauuwahhh.

I opened my eyes to see Bob had placed himself on the bed next to me with his face no more than a foot away from mine. His bright green eyes seemed to have an extra twinkle in them. It was nonsense to even think it, but it was as if he knew it was Christmas Day and was eager to get proceedings under way.

I had set the heating to come on early, just to warm the place up a bit. It was such a relief to get out of bed and find a little less of a chill in the air, especially given my poor circulation. I appreciated the warmth even more when I drew back the curtains to see the sky was still leaden and the trees once more coated with a layer of snow.

I put the kettle on and laid out some food for Bob. I then flicked on the little radio I had in the kitchen. It was playing suitably seasonal stuff – from Bing Crosby to Band Aid. It wasn't really my type of music but, without thinking about it, I found myself humming along. I was obviously in the mood.

The two of us had our own little routine on Christmas morning. Boxing Day with Belle was another affair, but today belonged to us. After breakfast, we began by popping outside to do his business.

I pressed on the lift button but nothing happened. Typical, I thought, of all the days to break down.

I could tell Bob wasn't happy walking down five flights of stairs. He knew that what went down had to go back up again.

I had written a card for Edna, the 'cat lady', who lived in a house across the road. She was always taking in waifs and strays and we often exchanged a few words, much to Bob's disgust. There were always a couple of cats perched on her wall or window ledge and he would often get agitated at the sight of them, arching his back as he stood on my shoulders.

It was too cold for them to be out today, however, so I popped the card through her letter box then headed back inside when Bob was finished.

The block of flats was as quiet as the grave. On the way back up the stairs I saw a guy who lived on the third floor, a bit of a rock 'n' roll sort of character with long hair and a leather jacket. He was obviously heading off somewhere for the day so we exchanged 'Merry Christmases'. Otherwise there wasn't a soul in sight. Clearly some people were home because I could smell the aroma of turkeys cooking in the ovens drifting up the stairwell. Bob smelled it too and started heading towards the landing of the fourth floor at one point, sniffing the air as he went.

'What's going on, Bob? Are you saying my cooking's not good enough for you?' I said, pulling a mock disappointed face.

Back in the flat Bob bounded up to the Christmas tree. It clearly needed to be inspected, in case it had miraculously moved or acquired an unacceptable new decoration while we were out. Once he'd satisfied himself that all was as it should be, he started sniffing around the presents. He studiously avoided Belle's piece of concrete this time, concentrating instead on the one that I'd wrapped in a special cat-themed Christmas paper.

'Well spotted, Bob,' I said, reaching in to extract it from under the tree then placing it next to me on the sofa.

He bounded down and was beside me in a flash.

His eyes were on stalks as I waved it around, his tail swishing around like it did when he was excited. When I put it next to him he began tearing at the paper and the ribbon, ripping them off the cardboard. I opened the box to reveal a wind-up toy with catnip inside that I'd been given by a regular in Covent Garden after we'd finished busking on Christmas Eve. He gave it a cursory look then picked up the cardboard box, held it briefly in his jaws, tossed it on to the floor and jumped down to play with it. It was a scene that, I was sure, was being re-enacted not just by cats but also by little children in many homes around the world.

'Who needs a present when the box is far more entertaining, eh?' I laughed.

Belle had given me a present to open on Christmas Day. From the shape of it, I guessed it was a second-hand video game that I'd been dropping hints about for a while. I knew that, unlike the new games which cost an absolute fortune, it was pretty inexpensive and that she could afford it. I opened it and was so excited that I spent the next hour or so setting it up and playing it a little. Bob was determined that I didn't get too involved, however. He was soon clambering over me and threatening to repeat the trick he'd pulled on a previous occasion where he switched the Xbox off altogether.

'OK, I get the picture, mate. It's time to get the Christmas dinner on.'

Bob's favourite thing to eat on Christmas Day is 'pigs in blankets', sausages wrapped in bacon. I love them too. So I put a packet of them in the oven to begin with. The distinctive whiff of cooked bacon was soon drifting through the air. I then peeled a few potatoes and stuck the small turkey crown I'd bought for myself in alongside them.

Bob had decided to take a brief nap by the radiator but the smells soon snapped him out of his slumber.

'Patience, mate,' I said, as he stuck his face a little too close to the oven door.

I brought out the 'pigs in blankets' first, placing the hot tray on the worktop. The sight and smell of them sent Bob into a complete frenzy. His tail was swishing around so fast that I wondered whether he might take off. He loved the bacon bits best so I dangled them in the air above him, teasing him a little as they cooled down. He was far too agile and quick for me, however. At one point he snatched a small rasher of bacon from my hand in the blink of an eye.

When everything was ready, I served the meal up on plates which I then put on a tray so we could eat on the sofa in front of the television. Bob always gobbled down his food as if there was no tomorrow but today he had competition in the speed-eating stakes. I don't think it took more than two minutes for both of us to clear our plates. The turkey was really tasty.

After clearing up I gave my family in south London a quick call on my mobile. Unfortunately it was just too complicated and difficult to get through to my mother in Australia but I spoke to my father for a few minutes. We weren't great conversationalists when we spoke on the phone. We wished each other a happy Christmas and asked each other about our plans for the day and the presents we'd been given. None of that took very long, in my case, at least. Being British, of course, we spent a sizeable chunk of the time talking about the weather. My father's van had got caught in a snowdrift the previous week, apparently. He'd had to dig his way out of the drift with his bare hands.

We talked for less than five minutes, but doing so made me feel better. The memory yesterday of that Christmas when he'd refused to talk to me had hurt. We probably weren't ever going to be the closest of fathers and sons. We rubbed each other up the wrong way, probably because we were so alike in many ways. He didn't like my lifestyle, I didn't like the fact that he constantly nagged me to get a haircut and 'a proper job', whatever one of those might be. But at least we had a relationship of sorts again and I was pleased about that.

Bob and I spent the rest of the day much as we'd spent the previous night, curled up on the sofa, me playing my new video game while he snored gently alongside me. Around the world millions of other people were probably enacting their idea of a perfect Christmas, maybe playing games, making music or simply eating, drinking and watching television. That was their idea. This had become ours. On a scale of 1 to 100 of contentment, Bob and I were at 101.

Boxing Day was, in many ways, the real Christmas Day for Bob and me. Just before lunchtime Belle arrived laden with four bulging supermarket bags full of food. The lift still wasn't working so when she rang the buzzer I walked down to help her carry the bags up. Bob trailed us all the way up the stairs, frantically trying to stick his head into the bags.

When we got back into the kitchen he jumped up on to the worktop to watch the unpacking.

'Here you go, mate,' Belle said, producing a slice of delicious-looking Spanish ham.

He grasped it in his teeth then lobbed it down on

to the floor where he ate it in seconds, wagging his tail excitedly as he did so.

Belle loves cooking and especially loves cooking a big Christmas roast then watching as everyone enjoys eating it. My kitchen wasn't the best equipped, but she soon had a small chicken, some roast potatoes and vegetables under way. It wasn't long before a new set of tasty aromas were wafting into the living room.

Every time Belle opened the oven Bob would sit bolt upright, sniff the air then scurry off into the kitchen, opportunistically looking for food.

'Not yet, mate,' she would say, closing the door again.

He would linger for a moment or two before giving up the ghost and limping back into the living room. It wasn't long before he was rewarded. There were soon bits of nicely cooked chicken being dispensed in his direction.

There was also a lovely smoked salmon starter for me and Belle along with some other nibbles. It felt like a five-star hotel.

It was around mid-afternoon when we finally ate, although we'd all been grazing on the various treats that Belle had brought for a couple of hours already. A lot of the stuff was excess from her mum and dad's Christmas Day meal, which was always a huge and lavish family affair. Today we ate on the small, fold-up table that I kept in the living room and Belle had dressed it up beautifully with serviettes and crackers. She'd laid three places, of course.

Bob didn't like the sound of the crackers so Belle and I pulled them a safe distance away from him as he lay on the living-room floor. We both put on a paper hat then Belle used some scissors and Sellotape to customise a hat for Bob so that he wasn't left out. We must have looked quite a picture, the three of us in our hats with our serviettes around our necks. It felt like we were a family, an unconventional one, but a family nevertheless.

I'd bought a small bottle of cava to toast the meal.

'Cheers,' I said, raising a glass to Belle. 'And thank you, for being such a great friend to Bob and me.' Bob sat on his chair unimpressed, far more interested in the small bowl of chicken that Belle had placed there for him.

I love Belle's cooking and I ate so much I could have burst. We had talked about going out for a walk, just to get some fresh air, but those plans were quickly discarded. Besides, it was colder than ever outside. We were far better off indoors.

I did the washing up and clearing away. By around 4 p.m. we were ready to sit down and open our presents.

Belle handed me an envelope first, smiling as she did so.

I opened it and pulled out a home-made card. It had a giant gold paw print on the front. The dedication inside simply said: *To James, from Belle and Bob*.

'That's one of the reasons why we made all that mess last weekend,' she giggled. 'I'd been making the card and he'd come over and deliberately placed his paw on it. It was going to be from just me, but he obviously wanted it to be from both of us.'

I was really touched and immediately gave it pride of place next to the tree.

Belle's parents were always generous and had given her a gift to pass on to me. It was a collector's edition of *The Rocky Horror Picture Show*, a favourite movie of mine.

I was still really apprehensive about Belle's gift. It had been the only minor cloud hovering over my Christmas Day. I kept trying to reassure myself that it would be OK. I knew her well enough to have got it right, I told myself. But I kept thinking that it could go either way. She would either be offended – or she'd love it. There couldn't really be a middle ground.

I took the present out from under the tree and gave it to her.

'Careful, it's heavy,' I said, feeling sheepish.

'Oh crikey, it is, isn't it?' she said when she took it off me.

She looked completely bewildered. It was an oddly shaped present. It obviously wasn't a book or a DVD or a bottle of perfume, or any of the normal presents that you might expect to receive at this time of the year. She clearly had no idea what it might be, which made it a success in one way already. But would she appreciate the surprise when she saw what it actually was?

I held my breath as she peeled the wrapping paper off, then took the piece of concrete in the palm of her hand and started looking at it.

'Wow,' she said.

I still wasn't quite sure how to take it. Did she mean *Wow, that's amazing*, or *Wow, what is this piece of rubbish that you've given me?*

She held it up and inspected it from every possible angle. I wasn't sure whether she was deliberately taking her time so as to torture me. I couldn't bear the tension any more.

'So go on, what do you think?'

'I think it's absolutely amazing, James.'

'You sure? You aren't just saying that to make me feel better about myself.'

'No. Absolutely not. It's great, where on earth did you get it?'

She laughed when I told her about the building site.

I felt so relieved. But I also felt slightly silly. Yes, the earrings I'd bought her were a lovely gesture. And I was sure she would have liked them. But I'd actually missed the point. We had never really been into buying each other expensive presents. For a start, we didn't have the money. But we also believed in giving each other things that meant something.

Our feeling was that it was not about the price tag on a present. It was about the love and thought that went into it, which was actually priceless. This odd little object that I'd stumbled across summed that up perfectly.

I had another present for her. I handed her an envelope marked 'Promises'.

Inside were half a dozen 'Promises' that I'd written out the previous night on pieces of coloured paper. They ranged from 'I Promise to cook you dinner' to 'I Promise to take you the cinema at least once in the next twelve months'. It was something we'd done before, especially at times like this when money was so scarce. Again we felt it had more meaning than an expensive 'bought' item. Belle really appreciated it, especially the cinema pledge. She loved going to see movies and it had been well over a year since I'd last taken her; I simply hadn't had the spare money.

For a moment we sat there, chatting and watching Bob as he played with the discarded wrapping paper and bows.

'He could do that for hours, couldn't he?' I smiled.

'Oh, nearly forgot,' Belle said, producing a small present from behind the tree. I hadn't seen it there before; she must have slipped it in when she'd arrived, without me noticing.

There was a tag attached. It read simply, *To James from Bob*.

I smiled at Belle.

'What's this?'

'Open it and you'll see.'

It was a small, plastic-covered photo album. The cover had the words 'Best Friends Forever' printed in large letters along with a picture of me and Bob, sitting on the pavement in Angel, selling *The Big Issue*. It must have been taken earlier that year, I reckoned. Inside Belle had pasted about a dozen photos of us together, going back to 2007 when I'd found him downstairs. There were snaps of us in the flat, on the bus and busking around Covent Garden. I recognised about half of them as pictures that Belle had taken herself with the camera on her phone. The other half were new to me, however. She told me she'd found a lot of them on the internet. There were now dozens of us on there, taken by people from all over the world. The best one, in which I was holding Bob close to my face, had been taken by a photography student who had asked me to do a photo shoot with him. He'd paid me a small fee then I'd forgotten all about it.

The album really touched me. Belle had obviously worked really hard on it and it contained a lot of images that made me feel quite emotional. As Boxing Day wore on, I couldn't stop looking at it.

Belle had brought a couple of DVDs over in case there was nothing we wanted to watch on television – neither of us were fans of the standard fare that tended to be shown at Christmas time. So after flicking through the channels and unsurprisingly finding nothing, we opted for one of the DVDs, *Scrooged* with Bill Murray. I wasn't a huge fan of the traditional versions of Dickens' *A Christmas Carol*, but loved this twisted take on the story of Scrooge in which Murray played a cynical television executive who is shown the error of his ways on Christmas Eve.

'It feels like my life this week,' I said as we watched his character visited by three ghosts, each representing his past, present and future.

Belle just laughed.

'Yeah right, James.'

Of course it was too corny to compare the past

week of my life to Scrooge's Christmas Eve. Yes I used to be pretty miserable at this time of the year, with good reason. But since I'd met Bob that had begun to alter. Thanks to him and Belle, I was learning to enjoy this time of year more and more.

There were some parallels though. There was no getting away from the fact that I'd had some thought-provoking encounters in the past few days, not just with the more charitable souls who approached me and Bob on the street, but with the other, darker figures who had crossed our paths.

There had been the drug dealer over in Soho, for instance. What was he? The Ghost of Christmas Past or the spirit of the present? As a recovering addict, the temptation of drugs was a part of my present and would be a part of my future too. And what about the young guy I'd seen sleeping in Monmouth Street? Was he the ghost of my past? I looked outside at the blackness and couldn't help wondering where he was right now. I hoped he had found somewhere safe and warm for the night.

I flicked back to the photo album that Belle had given me. She was sitting next to me on the sofa and Bob was draped across the pair of us. He was looking at the album too, as if he recognised himself.

Belle had arranged the photographs in chronological order, with the first in spring 2007 and the most recent just a few weeks ago, on Neal Street as we busked one evening. Flicking through the album, I could see what a different person I had been three years ago. I had been making real progress in my recovery at that point, but you could still tell that I had some way to go. My hair and skin looked different and I looked a lot less healthy. I looked a little lost, as if I wasn't quite with it all the time, which was probably true, even then, when I was a year or so into a methadone programme. I looked like a rather tortured and lonely soul, which is exactly what I was, of course. As I turned the pages, however, it was obvious that I was slowly, sometimes painfully slowly, getting healthier. You could see it in my eyes. I became more engaged, less haunted. But there was something else, something even more significant about me. I looked a happier, more stable person. And you could tell that from one simple detail in all the images. I was smiling.

It hit me when I looked at a photograph of me with Bob on my shoulder, posing for some tourists in Covent Garden. The tourists had big grins on their faces, but none of them were as big as mine. I was positively beaming, with what I recognised as a mixture of pride and simple joy. There were several photos where I was wearing the same expression. It was such a contrast.

If you'd made a photo album of my life during the previous ten years, you would have struggled to find many images like that. There probably weren't any. And a grin was the last thing you'd have seen. I didn't do much smiling during that lost decade.

The sequence of photos in the album was proof of something I'd known instinctively for a long time. These last three years had seen my life take such a change for the better, spiritually and emotionally. I had become a much lighter, more contented soul. There was no doubt that the steps I'd taken in my recovery from addiction were a huge element in that. But there was also no doubt that my world had improved because of the character sitting alongside me in all those photographs.

Until Bob had come along I'd been a hopeless cause. I'd wasted so many chances it was ridiculous. I was probably extremely lucky to be alive, such was the abuse I subjected my body to during my darkest days. The fact that I could now appreciate and enjoy a Christmas like this was just one of the blessings Bob had bestowed upon me. It was part of the even greater gift he had given me, probably the most wonderful one I'd ever received. Bob had given me a new life, a new life that was full of happiness and hope. As he, Belle and I curled up on the sofa that cold December night, I made another promise. I was going to treasure that gift, not just this Christmas, but for as long as we remained together.

Acknowledgements

To all of the wonderful hard-working charities we support, we hope each step of our journey continues to help you further.

Thank you to everyone involved in the making of the Bob books, without the behind-the-scenes 'Bobby Team' none of this would be possible. We would like to say thank you to Garry and Mary for making this a reality and bringing our story to life. To everybody at Hodder & Stoughton, Rowena, Kerry, Emma, Ciara, Maddy and Emily, you took a chance on us and for that we are eternally thankful. To my crucial and steadfast best friend and fundraising partner, Belle, Bob and I wouldn't be able to function without you in our lives!

And finally, there is one more huge thank you to

Bob. Bob will always be my constant companion through life. He taught me what no other could and I am indebted to him in this life and the next. But, of course, Bob and I have many more tales to tell before then.

Lots of love and hugs

James Bowen & Street Cat Bob